Ockham, Descartes, and Hume

Papers readied for press by
William J. Courtenay, William H. Hay, and Keith E. Yandell

Ockham, Descartes, and Hume

SELF-KNOWLEDGE, SUBSTANCE,
AND CAUSALITY

Julius R. Weinberg

The
University
of
Wisconsin
Press

Published 1977
The University of Wisconsin Press
Box 1379, Madison, Wisconsin 53701
The University of Wisconsin Press, Ltd.
70 Great Russell Street, London

First printing

Printed in the United States of America
For LC CIP information see the colophon

ISBN 0-299-072120-0

Publication of this book was made possible in part
by a grant from the Trustees of the William F. Vilas Trust Estate

Contents

Editors' Preface

No one who knew the late Julius Rudolph Weinberg could long remain unaware of the depth, breadth, and accuracy of his scholarship or of his philosophical acumen. His *Nicolaus of Autrecourt,* his "Ockham's Conceptualism" (selected as a Bobbs-Merrill reprint), and his 1970 Marquette University St. Thomas Aquinas Lecture, *Ideas and Concepts,* amply testify to his capacity for painstaking and exact research into the works of medieval philosophers. *A Short History of Medieval Philosophy* reveals the breadth of his knowledge of the philosophies of the medieval period, for in it his discusses Arabic, Jewish, and Christian sources, selecting for lucid discussion their central concepts and tenets. Though himself often in sharp disagreement with the philosophical views he discussed, these views, it is fair to say, rarely get as clear statement or as just a hearing as he consistently gave them. This includes his writings on the Rationalists and the Empiricists in his *Abstraction, Relation, and Induction* (though here too he traces many notions to their medieval settings), and his reply to Hintikka on the *cogito.* When one considers also his references to, and understanding of, the ancient philosophers, and the grasp of recent philosophy manifest in *An Examination of*

Logical Positivism and his various articles, it becomes clear that there was not much of the history of philosophy that escaped his scrutiny. The knowledge of the history of philosophy that he had at his finger tips was, in simple fact, truly extraordinary.

Professor Weinberg wrote much that he never offered for publication. Much of this remained fragmentary at his death, but there is a sizeable number of essays which in our judgment are of value to the scholarly world. This volume is then a last harvest of fruits of a mind with unusual range and accuracy. The papers included in Part I show him reporting on the results of his reading and examination of Latin texts of the medieval period; the firmness of his questioning and his command of the materials are seldom found together. Part II collects a recent set of papers which scrutinize some of the central claims of Descartes and of Hume.

In Part III we are presenting some papers on issues in what he called "systematic philosophy." For Julius Weinberg, unlike most other philosophers who have the historical discipline and the command of "the learned and vulgar tongues" needed to survey the monuments of Western philosophy, had a systematic philosophy in terms of which his historical analyses proceeded. It is therefore appropriate to make his statements of that philosophy available to readers. It is true that he had not himself offered them for publication, but we have judged that his own modesty in assessing his work should not prevent others from profiting by it.

Only a small part of the material here presented has been previously published. We have edited that as well as the unpublished manuscripts for accuracy and consistency of references and logical notation. It was an honor to be entrusted with this editorial work by his widow and a pleasure to perform it. We are grateful to her for her confidence in us and hope that the reader will concur in our judgment as to the value of the essays.

The editors wish to offer thanks for the assistance of John Vitale on identifying references, of David Fellman, Willard Hurst, and James Watrous for their encouragement and advice on bringing this collection to publication, and to express particular gratitude to the Trustees of the William F. Vilas Trust Estate for their financial support of the publication of this research done during Julius Weinberg's tenure of a Vilas Professorship.

There is special gratitude due to Janet Holt for her painstaking and accurate preparation of the typescript and to Mary Maraniss for her meticulous and helpful editing.

William J. Courtenay
William H. Hay
Keith E. Yandell

Madison, Wisconsin
1976

Acknowledgment

This volume is the outcome of several years of devoted effort by my late husband's friends and colleagues at the University of Wisconsin. I am deeply grateful to Professor William Courtenay of the Department of History, to Professor William H. Hay of the Department of Philosophy, and to Professor Keith E. Yandell of the Department of Philosophy for their faith in the value of these essays. I also want to thank their wives for the sacrifices they made in permitting their husbands to devote many long hours to the completion of this task. Mr. Thompson Webb, director of the University of Wisconsin Press, overcame numerous obstacles and tenaciously held to the goal of ultimate publication. And last but not least I want to thank our son, Mark P. Weinberg, for believing in the existence of materials not previously published and for assisting the editors in choosing the selections included in this volume. To all my heartfelt thanks.

Ilse H. Weinberg

December 1976

I
MEDIEVAL
PHILOSOPHY

1

The Argument of Anselm and Some Medieval Critics

I shall not be able to report much or perhaps anything about the ontological argument that is not already known to students of modern and contemporary philosophy. Pierre Gassendi rejected Descartes' version of the argument on the ground that *existence* is not a perfection.[1] Kant's general objection to most of the seventeenth-century versions,[2] and, more important, the discussions of Frege,[3] Russell,[4] and Moore,[5] have in my opinion settled the question once and for all. These several versions of the argument are, for two main reasons, radically unsound. Recent attempts by

1. Elizabeth S. Haldane and G. R. T. Ross, eds., *The Philosophical Works of Descartes*, 2 vols. (Cambridge: The University Press, 1911-12), II, 185 ff.
2. *Critique of Pure Reason*, B625.
3. Gottlob Frege, *The Foundations of Arithmetic: A Logico-Mathematical Enquiry into the Concept of Numbers*, trans. J. L. Austin (Evanston, Ill.: Northwestern University Press, 1968), p. 53.
4. Bertrand Russell, *Introduction to Mathematical Philosophy* (London, Allen and Unwin, New York, Macmillan, 1919), pp. 203 ff.
5. George E. Moore, *Philosophical Studies* (1922; Totowa, N.J.: Littlefield, Adams & Co., 1959), p. 197.

3

Professor Hartshorne[6] and Professor Malcolm[7] to defend the ontological argument have not changed this situation.

The best I can hope to do now is to explain Anselm's argument,
to exhibit several medieval variants, and to discuss some fourteenth-
century criticisms which anticipate remarkably the critique of Russell
and Moore. Anselm, while abbot of Bec, composed a number of
philosophical works (*De Veritate, De Libero Arbitrio, Monologion,
Proslogion*). In the preface of *Proslogion* the Saint tells us of his
intention: in the *Monologion*, the existence of God had been proved
by many arguments, but in this present work he wishes to produce
one argument for the existence of God that for its proof requires no
other than itself.

THE ARGUMENT OF *PROSLOGION*, CHAPTER 2

Faith assures us that God is something than which no greater can
be thought. But the Fool has said in his heart, "There is no God."

Now anyone hearing the expression *something than which nothing
greater can be thought* understands what he hears, and hence has in
mind what is referred to by this expression. Anselm assumes here
that to which the expression refers. So his preliminary argument is
this: If anyone understands a substantive expression, he has in mind
what this expression refers to. I understand the expression *that than
which no greater can be thought*, so its referent is in my mind. The
main argument now proceeds.

If T (that than which no greater can be thought) is not also *in
reality* as well as in my mind, then $T \neq T$ (i.e., that than which no
greater can be thought is *not* that than which no greater can be
thought); but as $T = T$, T is or exists in reality as well as in the mind.
He goes on, in chapter 3, to argue that God exists so truly that He
cannot even be conceived not to exist. For if T can be thought not
to exist, $T \neq T$; but as $T = T$, T cannot be thought not to exist. Later,
in Chapter 15, we find an even more remarkable consequence. God
must be even greater than can be thought. For if T is not greater

6. Charles Hartshorne, *The Logic of Perfection, and Other Essays in Neo-
classical Metaphysics* (LaSalle, Ill.: Open Court, 1962), ch. 2.

7. Norman Malcolm, "Anselm's Ontological Arguments," *Philosophical
Review*, 69 (1961).

than can be thought, $T \neq T$; but as $T = T$, T is greater than can be thought.

Unfortunately, though most learned medieval Christians would agree that the Divine nature transcends human comprehension, this last argument opens Anselm to a series of criticisms that seem to undermine his first argument and so to destroy his proof that there is a God. For if the supposed object referred to by the expression *that than which no greater can be thought* is actually beyond human comprehension, it is hard to see what Anselm could have meant by holding that when we understand the expression, we have its referent in mind—that is, that that than which no greater can be thought exists at least in our minds.

His attempts to extricate himself from this difficulty in his controversy with his first critic, Gaunilo, are not obviously successful:

> Even if were true that 'that than which a greater cannot be thought' cannot be thought of, it would not however be false that [the expression] 'than which a greater cannot be thought' can be thought of and understood. For just as nothing prevents one from saying 'ineffable' although one cannot specify what is said to be ineffable; and just as one can think of 'inconceivable' (although one cannot think of what 'inconceivable' applies to), so also, when 'than which a greater cannot be thought' is mentioned, there is no doubt at all that what is heard can be thought of and understood even if the thing itself cannot be thought of and understood.[8]

This, taken by itself, would seem to mean that what we understand when we hear the expression *than which a greater cannot be thought* is a singular description but not the referent of the description. Yet Anselm immediately adds:

> Whoever . . . denies that there is something than which a greater cannot be thought understands and thinks the denial he makes, and this denial cannot be understood apart from its elements [Quam negationem intelligere aut cogitare sine partibus eius]. Now one element of the denial is 'than

8. *Reply to Gaunilo,* ch. 9; see *St. Anselm,* ed. and trans. Sidney N. Deane (LaSalle, Ill.: Open Court, 1958), p. 168.

which a greater cannot be thought'. Whoever denies this understands and thinks of 'than which a greater cannot be thought'.[9]

That Anselm intends his readers to see that some object must be in the mind if we understand a sentence with a subject term is stated emphatically.

> For just as what is thought is thought by means of a thought, and what is thought by a thought is then, as thought, *in thought*, so also what is understood is understood by the mind, and what is understood by the mind is thus, as understood, in the mind.[10]

Gaunilo (994–1083?), who engaged Anselm in this controversy, was an abbot of Marmoutier, near Tour. His critique of Anselm's argument must have been written about 1078. He argues, first of all, "that this thing is said already to exist in my mind, only in the sense that I understand what is said. For could I not say that all kinds of unreal things not existing in themselves in any way at all, are likewise in the mind since if anyone speaks of them I understand what is said?"[11] In the case of an artist who is said to have in mind what he has not yet made, such a thing said to be *in mind* is identical with the knowledge of understanding of the mind itself. On the other hand, in the case of any truth perceived by the mind, "it cannot be doubted that this truth is one thing and the mind which grasps it another thing."[12] Gaunilo pursues this line of thought further: "Therefore, when I hear and understand someone who says that there is something greater than everything that can be thought of, it is agreed that it is in the sense of one not really knowing the object, but thinking of it in terms of an affection of his mind produced by the spoken words that it is in my mind and not in any other sense."[13]

Gregory of Rimini, a theologian of the fourteenth century, developed Gaunilo's criticism on this point. Before I turn to later

---

9. Ibid.
10. Ibid.
11. *Appendix in Behalf of the Fool*, sec. 1; see Deane, *St. Anselm*, p. 146.
12. *Appendix*, sec. 3; see Deane, p. 147.
13. *Appendix*, sec. 4; see Deane, p. 149.

criticisms of the argument, however, I should like to show how the argument was developed among some thirteenth-century theologians. I pass over the twelfth century, since there is no evidence which has yet turned up that Anselm's argument was used or discussed until the thirteenth.

ORIGINS OF THE ARGUMENT

Sources of the expression *id quo maior nihil cogitare potest* as a description of God are:

a. Seneca, *Quaestiones naturales*, I, Preface 13. "What is God? That than which no greater can be cogitated."

b. Augustine, *Confessions*, VI, 4. "For never yet was, nor will be, a soul able to conceive of anything better than Thou, who art the biggest and best good."

c. Augustine, *On the Morals of the Manicheans*, ch. 11, no. 24. "That God is the supreme good, and that than which nothing can be or be conceived better, we must either understand or believe, if we wish to keep clear of blasphemy."

d. Augustine, *On Christian Doctrine*, I, 7, 7. "For when the supreme God of gods is thought of, even by those who believe that there are other gods,..., their thought takes the form of an attempt to reach the conception of a nature, than which nothing more excellent or exalted exists."

e. Boethius, *The Consolation of Philosophy*, vol. 3, ch. 10. "For, since nothing can be imagined better than God, who doubts but that is good than which is nothing better?" ("Nam cum nihil deo melius excogitare queat, id quo melius nihil est bonus esse quis dubitet?")

Sources of the principle *If I understand an expression, its meaning is in my mind* are:

a. Aristotle, *De Interpretationes*, ch. 1, 16^23. "Spoken sounds are symbols of affections in the soul and written marks are symbols of spoken sounds; spoken and written sounds differ for different peoples, but what these are the signs of—the affections of the soul—are the same for all, and their referents—the actual things—are also the same."

b. Augustine, *Confessions*, X, 15, 23. "Yet unless its image were present in my memory, I would not know what I am talking about, and I would not distinguish it from pleasure in a discussion."

Sources of the notion of God as *Being* are:

a. Exodus 3 : 14. "I am who am." ("Ego sum, qui sum.")

b. Augustine (*De Civites Dei*, XII, 2, and *De Trinitate*, V, 2, 3) describes God as the "highest essence" and as one who exists in the highest degree, "who possesses being in a higher degree than life, who said to his servant Moses 'I am who am' and 'He who is, has sent me to you' . . . . Therefore, only the essence of God, or the essence which God is, is unchangeable. Being is in the highest and truest sense of the term proper to Him from whom being derives its name. . . . Only that which is not only not changed, but cannot undergo any change at all, can be called being in the truest sense without any scruple."

Anselm does not hesitate to characterize God as existing through Himself ("existendi per se," *Monologion* ch. 3), and the statement that it is greater to be both in mind and in reality than in the mind alone shows that Anselm accepts some version of the degrees-of-reality doctrine. And (in *Proslogion*, ch. 5) Anselm expressly states that God exists through Himself alone. God is the highest of all things existing through Himself. God is whatever He is, not through another being but through His very self (*Proslogion*, ch. 12). All the divine attributes are thus identical with the divine being.

In William of Auxerre's *Summa Aurea* (composed between 1215 and 1231) we find the following argument: "When I say *highest good, or best* I understand all good attributes. Now since *being* is such a good which all desire it follows that this very being [ipsum esse] is understood in what I call *the best* or the *highest good.* Now whatever is contained follows from what contains it. . . . Since *being* is contained in the *best,* being follows from *the best.* . . . So it follows that if the best is intelligible the best exists, but as it is certain that the best is intelligible, the best consequently exists." This, as will be immediately recognized, is an ontological argument somewhat different from Anselm's argument, which William also states without essential modification.

Richard Fishacre (d. 1248) repeated Anselm's argument in his *Sentence-Commentary*,[14] as did Alexander of Hales (d. 1245).[15] We turn to St. Bonaventure (d. 1274) for a further development. He repeats Anselm's second argument (from *Proslogion*, ch. 3) in his *Disputed Questions on the Mystery of the Trinity*,[16] as well as Anselm's first argument. But he then formulates the argument in a different way: If God is God, God exists. The antecedent is so true that it cannot be thought not to be; so that God exists is indubitably true. Still another formulation: That God exists is guaranteed as self-evident because the predicate of *God exists* is contained in the subject.

Bonaventure's pupil Matthew of Aquasparta, in the *Disputed Questions on the Production of Things*,[17] elucidates Bonaventure's argument more fully: If the best is the best, the best exists, since *the best* means inter alia the most actual and complete being and so being in act. So it follows of necessity that if the first and highest is the first and highest, then the first and highest exists, because the first and highest is the most complete act and by virtue of this it exists in act.

These are some but not all of the main variants of the ontological argument. The form of the argument which holds that the existence of God can be inferred from His essence owes a great deal to a distinction between existence and essence in finite beings and the identity of existence and essence in God. This latter notion was introduced into medieval thought by the Persian philosopher Avicenna (d. 1037), some of whose writings were translated into Latin in the twelfth century. According to Avicenna, the essence or nature of any finite being is what is presented in its definition. A definition simply states the constituent elements of such a nature, what it is to be; for example, a horse, etc. From such a definition we cannot tell whether or not there are horses. So the existence of any such must be an accident added to the essence. Only in God is there no difference between essence and existence. God is a necessary being; that

---

14. See P. Augustinus Daniels, *Quellenbeitrage und Untersuchungen zur Geschichte der Gottesbeweisa im 13: Jahrhundart* (Münster, 1909), p. 24.
15. *Summa Theologiae*, Quaracchi ed., vol. 1, sec. 25. See Daniels, p. 27.
16. *De Mysterio Trinitatis*, I, 1, 9.
17. See Daniels, pp. 159-61.

is, the denial of his existence implies a contradiction.[18] A possible being, on the other hand, can be assumed to exist or not without any contradiction resulting. And in a possible being, essence is different from existence, which is added to the possible being when it comes to exist.

This distinction was widely accepted in various forms among the medieval Christian theologians. But it was sharply attacked and rejected by Averroes in the twelfth century and by William of Ockham in the fourteenth century.

Aquinas devised a subtle version of the distinction of essence and existence and so maintained that *God exists* is, in itself, a necessary and self-evident truth. But, as far as human intelligence functioning in this world is concerned, the proposition is not self-evident. According to Aquinas, all human knowledge results from sensation, from which the mind abstracts the essence of material things. The knowledge of nonmaterial things must be inferred from the existence and behavior of those material things and processes which are accessible to human perception. Now this means that since in the present life we have no direct knowledge of the divine nature, the proposition *God exists* is not self-evident. So when Anselm holds that *God* means that than which nothing greater can be thought and infers his existence from this description, Thomas replies that "even if everyone understands that by the name *God* is signified that than which nothing greater can be thought, it does not follow from this that what the name signifies exists actually but only that it exists mentally. It cannot be argued that it actually exists, unless it is admitted that there really is something than which nothing greater can be thought; and it is precisely this that is not admitted by those who hold that God does not exist."[19]

The exact force of this criticism is not as clear as it might be unless we are permitted to suppose that Aquinas, by denying that we have a notion of the Divine Essence, is denying that Anselm's expression is more than a description. In any case, far subtler criticisms are to be found in the nominalists of the fourteenth century.

Robert Holcot, in his *Quodlibetal Question* "Whether theology is a science?" argues that Anselm begs the question.

18. *Metaphysices Compendium*, B1, part 2, cap. 1.
19. *Summa Theologiae*, Part I, q. 2, a. 1, reply obj. 2.

if he supposed that there is such a being than which a greater cannot be thought; or, if Anselm does not assume this, then since he proves that no such exists, he proves nothing to the purpose.

For, when Anselm holds that that than which a greater cannot be thought does not merely exist in the mind, I say that this is implicative of the false. Since it is nothing, because a greater than it can be thought, if I say that every being is of finite power and finite both intensively and extensively, as any infidel may wish to assert.[20]

I think that Holcot wishes to say that, granting that every being whatsoever is finite in power, one can think the description *that than which no greater can be conceived*, but the description will then describe nothing.

Holcot attacks another aspect of the argument. In Anselm's second argument (*Proslogion*, ch. 3), as well as in the formulation of Bonaventure and Matthew of Aquasparta, appeal was made to the principle that *A is the same as A* is always true. Boethius had written, in his *Commentary on De Interpretatione*,[21] that no proposition is truer than that in which the same thing is predicated of itself. Now, Ockham and later Holcot challenged this principle. It applies, they held, provided that there is something corresponding to the subject term, but otherwise not, because then it implies a falsehood. Thus *A chimaera is a chimaera* implies that there is a chimaera, which is false. Similarly, if there were no white men, *A white man is white* would be false.

The application to the problem here is this: when it is said that God is God, this is not a necessary truth, if *God* means "the best" or "that than which a greater cannot be thought" or "that which is unlimited in power" or the like. A point of logic will help us understand what is involved here. If we succeed in naming something and then in using the name, say *a*, that we have assigned it, we can say *a is identical with a.* For this will mean *Every attribute of a is an attribute of a,* which is certainly true. Or if we have such indirect knowledge that there is something which has some specified attri-

20. *Quodlibetal Questions*, I, Ms Pembroke College, Cambridge 236, fol. 195^r.

21. *In Librum Aristotelis*, II, PL64, col. 387c5.

bute, say *P*, we can say $(\exists x)(Px \cdot x = x)$, from which $(\exists x)(x = x)$ follows, which is certainly true.

Moreover, even if an attribute is known not to belong to anything, we can infer from $\sim(\exists x)(Px)$ that $(\exists A)(A = P \cdot \sim(\exists x)Ax)$. But the statement that at least one chimaera is a chimaera or the statement that the only griffin = the only griffin will be false if there are no chimaeras and no griffins (or, of course, more than one).

The appeal to the law of identity is, on this theory at least, vain. Gregory of Rimini devised a different criticism which may be regarded as a development of Gaunilo's first objection to Anselm.

Anselm argued that whatever is understood is *in* the mind. But, taken generally, this principle must be false. To show its falsity let us consider the following. The verbal expression *that which cannot be thought* can be thought. But it does not follow from this that that which cannot be thought can be thought. For the latter is a contradiction, and if it followed from the former, it too would be a contradiction, which plainly it is not.

Another example. The verbal expression *a greater than that than which a greater cannot be thought* can be thought. But it does not follow that anyone can think of something greater than that than which a greater cannot be thought.

Someone might argue as follows. The statement *A being greater than God cannot exist* is intelligible and true. But the subject of the statement is *a greater than God.* So, if the whole statement is understood, the subject is understood. But Gregory denies that we can always suppose that the subject expression of every statement stands for something. In the statement *What cannot be thought cannot be thought*, the subject expression does not stand for anything. So it is not generally the case that in order to understand a whole statement it is necessary that every (or any) part of it has a referent peculiar and proper to itself.

Now if all this is sound, the first argument of Anselm does not, as we say, get off the ground. If the expression *that than which no greater can be thought* can be understood without supposing that it even has so much as an intramental referent, Anselm's argument cannot get started. And this seems to vindicate some of the objections of Gaunilo.

I have not discussed the objection that *exists* cannot be a characterizing predicate. This argument was brought against Descartes' formulation of the ontological argument by Gassendi and, later, by Kant. It is worth mentioning that Averroes and Ockham also brought this argument against some medievals who had supposed otherwise.

I myself am convinced that *exists* cannot be construed as a characterizing predicate. But even if this were mistaken, the weakness of Anselm's first argument makes it clear that, as older writers put it, only ideal existence is involved in the description *that than which a greater cannot be thought.* And this, by itself, is enough to destroy the cogency of the *Ratio Anselmi.*

This is why both Spinoza and Malebranche were wiser to hold that the divine nature is conceived in itself. I believe they were wrong in supposing we confront infinite being in our thought. But only if we were vouchsafed such an experience would the existence of such a being be assured.

It is worth something to call attention to a remarkable similarity between the conclusions of Ockham, Holcot, and Rimini, on the one hand, and those of Russell, on the other.

According to Russell, a descriptive phrase of the form *the so-and-so* (e.g., *the man who broke the bank at Monte Carlo, the author of the Iliad, the King of Jordan*) has meaning only as part of a larger context and does not have an independent meaning as, for instance, a proper name might be supposed to have an independent meaning.

The main contexts in which such phrases occur are

$$E!(\imath x)(\varphi x) \text{ and } \varphi(\imath x)(\varphi x)$$

which can be defined as follows:

$$E!(\imath x)(\varphi x) =_{\text{def}} (\exists x)[\varphi x \cdot (y)(\varphi y \supset y = x)]$$

$$\varphi(\imath x)(\varphi x) =_{\text{def}} (\exists x)[\varphi x \cdot (y)(\varphi y \supset y = x)]$$

Accordingly,

$$\varphi(\imath x)(\varphi x) \equiv (\exists x)[\varphi x \cdot (y)(\varphi y \supset y = x) \cdot \varphi x]$$
$$\equiv (\exists x)[\varphi x \cdot (y)(\varphi y \supset y = x)]$$
$$\equiv E!(\imath x)(\varphi x)$$

and

$$[(\imath x)(\varphi x) = (\imath x)(\varphi x)] \equiv$$

$$(\exists x)[\varphi x \cdot (y)(\varphi y \supset y = x) \cdot ((\exists_z)[\varphi_z \cdot (y)(\varphi y \supset y = z)] \equiv$$

$$(\exists x)[\varphi x \cdot (y)(\varphi y \supset y = x) \cdot \varphi x] \equiv$$

$$(\exists x)[\varphi x \cdot (y)(\varphi y \supset y = x)] \equiv$$

$$(E!(\imath x)(\varphi x).$$

Now, this certainly justifies (a) the claim of Gregory of Rimini that the understanding of a descriptive statement does not require a referent for the subject-term of the statement, and (b) the claims of Ockham and Holcot that not all statements involving identity expressions are logical truths, and finally (c) the claims of Averroes and Ockham that *existence* is not some accident distinct from essence in creatures and identical with essence in the case of God.

2

Gregory of Rimini's Critique of Anselm

The usual criticisms of Anselm's argument have been concerned with the inference from the content of the concept of God to His existence, and doubtless much has been learned from the many discussions of this topic. A reexamination of Anselm's argument and a consideration of Gregory of Rimini's critique throw another light on the argument which is of some interest.

In chapter 2 of *Proslogion*, Anselm presented an argument consisting of two parts. The first part: Anyone hearing the expression *that than which nothing greater can be thought* understands what he hears and therefore has in his mind what is referred to by this expression. Thus if anyone understands a substantive expression, he has in mind what this expression refers to. Now, I understand *that than which no greater can be thought*. It follows that the referent of the expression is in my mind. The second part: Put *T* for *that than which nothing greater can be conceived*. Then if *T* is not also *in reality* (in *re*), *T* is not *T*; but as *T* is *T*, *T* exists in reality as well as in the mind.

We shall be concerned only with what I have called the first part of the argument. But it is just as well to notice a consequence

15

Anselm draws in chapter 15 of the *Proslogion* which tends to under-mine what has been alleged in chapter 2. For, in chapter 15 it is argued that God must be greater than can be thought, because if *T* is not greater than can be thought, then *T* is not *T*, a consequence which, evidently, Anselm regards as intolerable. It is true, of course, that he recoils from the obvious consequences of this in his reply to Gaunilon.[1]

Anselm says, in this reply, two things. First of all:

> Even if it were true that that than which a greater cannot be thought cannot be thought of (or understood), it would not, however, be false that [the formula] 'that-than-which-a-greater-cannot-be-thought' could be thought of and under-stood. For just as nothing prevents one from saying 'ineffable' although one cannot specify what is said to be ineffable, and just as one can think of 'inconceivable', although one cannot think of what 'inconceivable' applies to—so also, when 'that-than-which-a-greater-cannot-be-thought' is spoken of, there is no doubt at all that what is heard can be thought of and understood even if the thing itself cannot be thought of and understood.[2]

But Anselm immediately adds to this a second statement which might seem to contradict it, if we did not notice that the statement just quoted was in the imperfect subjunctive:

> Whoever . . . denies that there is something than which a greater cannot be thought understands and thinks the denial he makes, and this denial cannot be understood apart from its elements.[3] Now one element of the denial is 'than which a greater cannot be thought'.

That Anselm intends us to see that some object must be in the mind if we understand a sentence with a subject is stated with some emphasis:

1. *Contra Insipient.* The translations of Anselm are all those of M. J. Charlesworth, *St. Anselm's Proslogion with a Reply on Behalf of the Fool by Gaunilo and the Author's Reply to Gaunilo* (Oxford: Oxford University Press, 1965).
2. Charlesworth, p. 187.
3. "Quam negationem intelligere aut cogitare sine partibus eius."

> For just as what is thought is thought by means of a thought,
> and what is thought by a thought is then, as thought, *in*
> thought, so also what is understood is understood by the
> mind, and what is understood by the mind is then, as under-
> stood, in the mind.[4]

Now all this was said in reply to Gaunilon's first objection, which
was to the following effect:

> . . . that this thing is said already to exist in my mind, only in
> the sense that I understand what is said. For could I not say
> that all kinds of unreal things not existing in themselves in
> any way at all, are likewise in the mind since if anyone speaks
> of them I understand what is said?"[5]

Whether Anselm's replies to this critique are satisfactory or even
coherent can, perhaps, be better determined in the light of the discussion of Gregory of Rimini. But before we get on to this, another
preliminary will be useful.

We may wonder what, historically, lies back of Anselm's assumption, "If I understand an expression, its meaning is in my mind."
There are at least two texts he undoubtedly studied which state
similar doctrines. One is Aristotle's *De Interpretatione*, which in
chapter 1, 16^{a}3 expresses the view that "spoken sounds are symbols
of affections in the soul and written marks are symbols of spoken
sounds; spoken and written sounds differ for different people, but
what these are signs of—the affection of the soul—are the same for
all and their referents—the actual things—are also the same." And
Augustine in *Confessions*, X, 15, 23, held that "unless its image were
present in my memory, I would not know what I am talking about,
and I would not distinguish it from pleasure in a discussion." It is
such opinions as these, then, which seem to be back of Anselm's
assumption. And it is chiefly this assumption which will be
questioned.

Gregory of Rimini, writing his *Questions on the Sentences*, chs.
42, 43, q. 3, a. 3 (c. 1344)[6] asked "whether by following natural

4. Charlesworth, p. 184.
5. Ibid., p. 157.
6. [Professor Weinberg translated Rimini's critique of Anselm and included

reason it must be held that God is of infinite intensive power?" Since he and fourteenth-century theologians assumed that Anselm's *that than which no greater can be thought* is equivalent to *something of infinite intensive power*, he was obliged to take up and to evaluate Anselm's argument.

The critique of Gregory is here confined to the first part of Anselm's argument: he holds that it is simply mistaken to say that whatever one understands is in the mind. Thus the argument: *that than which a greater cannot be thought* is understood, hence *that than which a greater cannot be thought is understood* is unsound. For if it were a sound argument, so also would be the following argument: *What cannot be thought* can be thought; hence what cannot be thought can be thought. But this argument cannot be sound, for its premise is plainly consistent and true, and its conclusion is self-contradictory. So in any case, the alleged conclusion cannot follow.[7] Moreover, *a greater than that than which a greater cannot be thought* is understood. But it surely does not follow from this that a greater than that than which a greater cannot be thought is understood.[8]

---

it in *Problems in Philosophical Inquiry* (New York: Holt, Rinehart and Winston, 1971), pp. 499–501.—Eds.]

7. If *P* yields *Q* is a contradiction, then *P* is a contradiction. Now if *P* is not a contradiction and Q is a contradiction, then P cannot yield Q.

8. Gregorii Ariminensis, O.E.S.A., *Super Primum et Secundum Sententiarum*, fol. 170 v., Q, The Franciscan Institute, St. Bonaventure (New York: 1955). "Cum dicitur aliquid esse in intellectu, si pro eodem accipiatur ac si dicitur quod illus intelligitur, concedo propositionem, sed nihil est ad propositum quia audiens illam utique intelligit illam et illa intelligitur ab eo. Sed non sequitur: haec vox 'aliquid quo maius cogitari non potest intelligitur, si subjectum consequentis supponat significative'. Sicut etiam non sequitur: haec vox 'quod non potest cogitari' potest cogitari, ergo quod non potest cogitari potest cogitari. Nam antecedens est verum, quoniam audiens hoc quod dico (quod non potest cogitari) cogitat quod audit, et quod ipse cogitat cogitatur, et tamen consequens implicat contradictionem si subjectum supponat significative. Similiter audiens hanc vocum: 'maius eo quo maius cogitari non potest' intelligit quod audit, et ipsa vox intelligitur ab eo, et tamen non sequitur: haec vox 'maius eo quo maius cogitari non potest' intelligitur, erto maius eo quo maius cogitari non potest intelligitur. Nam antecedens est verum, et consequens (si subjectum supponat significative) est falsum etiam secundum Anselmum. Non ex ipso sequitur quod eo quod maius cogitari non potest aliquid maius cogitari potest quod ipse dicit esse impossibile in prima probatione 2^{ae} partis antecedentis et contra insipienti.

The result of these considerations is simply that we cannot suppose that there is a referent for every substantive term of discourse, and from this it immediately follows that the first part of Anselm's argument has not been proved. It is plain that, insofar as the second part of the argument depends on the first part, Anselm's case has not been made. And this for reasons quite different from the usual criticisms; for example, that *exists* cannot be a characterizing predicate.

Gregory offers a solution for the difficulties. Not every term can be taken to stand for something which appears to be signified by the term in question. He expresses surprise that Anselm himself had conceded this point in his tract *On the Fall of the Devil.*[9]

Now what holds for *nothing* and *not-something* holds as well for expressions such as *unthinkable, that which cannot be thought*, and *that than which a greater cannot be thought*. John of Mirecourt presented the following argument: A greater than God can be thought; nothing greater than God can be thought; hence, a greater can be thought than that than which no greater can be thought.

According to Gregory,[10] Mirecourt attempted to prove this curious argument as follows: Whoever thinks the proposition *A greater*

9. Anselm; *De Casu Diaboli*, Cap. XL. [quomodo malum et nihil non possint probari per nomen suum aliquid esse: sed quasi aliquid.]

"Magister: Recte quaeris, quia licet supraposita ratione, malum et nihil significent aliquid: tamen quod significatur malum non est, aut nihil, sed et alia ratio, qua significant aliquid: et quod significatur est aliquid, sed none vere est aliquid: sed quasi aliquid. Multa quidem dicuntur secundum formam, quae non sunt secundum rem, ut timere, secundum forman vocis dicitur activum, cium sit passivum secundum rem. Ita quoque caecitas, dicitur aliquid secundum forman loquendi, cum non sit aliquid secundum rem.

"Multa quoque alia similiter dicuntur aliquid secundum forman loquendi, quae non sunt aliquid: quoniam sic loquimur de illus sicut de rebus existentibus."

See also the translation of Jasper Hopkins and Herbert Richardson, *Anselm of Canterbury: Truth, Freedom and Evil* (New York: Harper Torchbooks, 1967), pp. 163–68.

10. This refers to the doctrine for which Gregory of Rimini is best known, that the object of knowledge is not the conclusion of the demonstration but rather the total and adequate signification of the conclusion, which is also called an "enunciable" or "that which can be signified by a proposition" (*complexe significabile*). The term "propositio," in medieval discussions, refers always to a spoken sentence, a written sentence, or a sentence which is thought. So in the twelfth century, the referents of such sentences are called by Abelard

than God cannot exist understands a true statement. Now in order to understand such a statement one must understand its principal part. The principal part of *A greater than God cannot exist* is the expression *a greater than God.* Hence *a greater than God* can be thought. On the other hand, nothing greater than God can be thought, because of every instance which can be presented, we must say that it is not greater than God.

The main objection to this sort of argument is put by Gregory of Rimini in these terms:

> I concede that he who thinks 'A greater than God cannot exist' thinks a truth. . . . But when it is further inferred that such a person thinks of a Greater than God, I deny that this follows. With regard to the proof by which he [Mirecourt] argues that 'a greater than God' is the principal part of the truth in question, I say that this is false if the subject [i.e., 'a greater than God'] supposits personally. . . . For . . . it is clear that it is false to assert that 'a greater than God' is a part of the enunciation 'A greater than God cannot exist'. If the truth here is understood to be that which can be enunciated or that which is signified by the enunciation, granting that it is somewhat improper, it may be allowed that what is signified by the subject is a part of the total significate, and so is, in some way, thought. I say that in 'A greater than God cannot exist', the partial significate neither stands for something other than 'a greater than God' nor need it stand for anything at all, because the statement is negative. The same applies in the case of the statement 'What cannot be thought cannot be thought' which is a true statement: the subject, in this example, stands for no thing.[11]

"dicta propositionum," and in the fourteenth century by Gregory of Rimini they are called "enunciabilia," "totalia significata conclusionum," or "complexe significabilia." The doctrine was rejected by Buridan, Pierre d'Ailly, Marsilius of Inghen, and many others.

No doubt, Gregory's critique of Mirecourt is difficult to render consistent with his doctrine of "complexe significabilia," but note that he says that it could only be said "is properly" that the phrase "maius deo" refers to a part of what is signified by the whole proposition "maius deo non potest esse." On this subject, see H. Elie, *Le Complexe Significabile* (Paris, 1937).

11. Gregorii Ariminensis O.E.S.A., *Super Primum et Sedundum Sententiarum*, fol. 171, H. ". . . concedo quod quia cogitat de isto (maius deo non

From this it can be gathered that the critic is feeling his way toward a theory of meaning which does not require each substantive part of a statement to have a referent in order that the entire statement be meaningful and even true. The full elaboration of such a theory requires a theory of quantifiers which logicians did not achieve until the nineteenth century, but some of the reasons for such a theory have evidently been intimated by Gregory of Rimini.

If the core of this criticism is sound, the main argument of Anselm cannot get off the ground. For, if the expression *that than which a greater cannot be thought* can be understood as a part of a statement without supposing that it necessarily has any peculiar and proper referent, even an intracognitive referent, the main argument of Anselm cannot be stated.

These reflections of Gregory of Rimini would seem to elucidate and vindicate the first objection of Gaunilo. They may have been suggested by reflection on Anselm's argument by earlier fourteenth-century theologians, and I cannot, with any assurance, guarantee that they originated with Gregory. But, whoever is ultimately responsible for them, they constitute a brilliant piece of philosophical analysis.

---

potest esse verum cogitat: et verum cogitatur ab eo. Sed cum ulterius infertur 'ergo maius deo cogitatus ab eo', si in isto consequente subjectum supponat materialiter, concedo consequens sed nihil ad propositum. Si vero personaliter, nego consequentiam. Et ad probationem qua dicitur quod maius deo est maxima pars illius veri, dico etiam quod ista est falsa, si subjectum supponat personaliter et hoc qualitercumque accipiatur verum cum dicitur quod verum cogitatur ab eo.

"Nam si accipiatur pro ipsa enuntiatione vera, hac, scilicet (maius deo non potest esse), patet quod ista est falsa *'maius deo* est pars enunciationis huius' maius deo non potest esse. Si vero accipiatur verum pro enuntiabile seu significato illius enuntiationes verae, quamvis alique modo licet improprie posset concedi quod significati totalis, et aliquo modo cogitatum. Dico quod pro illo significato partiali nec pro aliquo alio supponit in ista 'maius deo non potest esse', nec oportet quod pro aliquo supponat, cum ista sit negativa; sicut in ista quae utique vera est, 'quod non potest cogitari, non potest cogitari', subjectum pro nullo supponit."

3

Ockham's Theory of Scientific Method

There can be no doubt that Ockham recognized a principle of causality as somehow self-evident. His use of terms was extremely precise, and he was unusually acute in discerning and removing the ambiguities of philosophical words. Since he held that there is a sufficient proof (*sufficienter probari*)[1] or demonstration (*potest demonstrari Deumesse*)[2] that there is a First Conserver, and since *demonstration* has a very precise significance in his philosophy, we may be sure that Ockham recognized as self-evident some "causal" principle in demonstration.[3]

1. *Ordinatio in Librum Primum Sententiarum*, dist. 2, q. 10, in *Opera Philosophica et Theologica. Opera Theologica*, vol. II (St. Bonaventure, N.Y.: Franciscan Institute, 1970), pp. 354–57, 342–46; *Quaestiones in Physicam*, qq. 132–36.

2. *Quodlibeta Septem*, i, q. 1.

3. E. Hochstetter, *Studien zur Metaphysik und Erkenntnislehre Wilhelms von Ockham* (Berlin, 1927), p. 145: "Das Prinzip [i.e., principle of causality] hat vielmehr auch für ihn unbedingte Gültigkeit, soweit seine Leugnung zu der Konsequenz führt, dass etwas in derselben Beziehung zugleich Ursache und Wirkung seiner selbst ist, was ein Widerspruch wäre." As Hochstetter remarks, Ockham makes one exception in connection with the spontaneity of the volitional act. Hence, *Ordinatio*, dist. 35, q. 2, C: ". . . quamvis probetur quod

Ockham also explicitly stated that the principle that like causes have like effects is self-evident.[4]

Yet Ockham was perfectly sure that any given causal generalization is neither evident in itself nor capable of demonstration.[5] His reasons show a remarkable insight into the difference between logic and mathematics on the one hand and natural science on the other. Specifically, he recognized (1) that it is universally the case that the prediscursive[6] acquaintance with one thing is never sufficient for the prediscursive knowledge of another thing, (2) that a thing does not always contain its "passion" actually or virtually, and (3) that the knowledge of a thing and its "passion" does not always suffice for knowing a proposition composed of the names of the thing and its "passion." In other words, the discovery of the causal characteristics of things requires more than either logic or the acquaintance with the terms of a proposition. Thus,

> However often one experiences in himself that he knows something perfectly and intuitively, he will never by so knowing a thing, know another thing unless he has previous knowledge of that other thing. . . . If you say that if a subject were cognized according to its whole being then all its "passions" would be cognized, this does not hold. For in order to cognize a cause *sub rationae causae* presupposes a knowledge of that thing which is the effect . . . hence the

---

primum efficiens est nobilius omni effectu, tamen non probatur quod est nobilius omni alio ente, quia non probatur sufficienter quod omne ens est efficiens vel effectus alicuius efficientis." But does not Hochstetter realize that this is a very serious concession? And does he not also realize that the dialectical proof of a principle of causality he imputes to Ockham is either useless or a *petitio principii*?

4. *Reportatio in Librum Secundum Sententiarum*, II, q. 25, L: ". . . omnes formae eiusdem rationis possunt habere effectus eiusdem rationis."

5. *Summa Logicae*, III, pt. 2, ch. 12; *Ordinatio*, Prol., q. 2, in *Opera Theologica*, I, 86-87.

6. I use the word *prediscursive* to render *notitia incomplexa*. This is not strictly accurate. The scholastics generally recognized three stages of knowledge: (1) simple acquaintance with things, qualities, etc.; (2) propositions; and (3) inference. Here *prediscursive* means simple acquaintance with a thing prior to the formation of propositions or the performance of inferences.

24   *Ockham, Descartes, and Hume*

knowledge of a thing *sub ratione causae* is not so much the reason for knowing the effect as the result of knowing the effect.[7]

In brief, *experience* of causal routines is an indispensable condition of knowing causal generalizations. Yet Ockham also maintains that evident knowledge of causal generalizations can be obtained from experience.

It is the purpose of this discussion to expound and evaluate the theory of science by which Ockham thought to establish a universal causal generalization on a finite (and, ideally, a very small) number of instances. The assumptions on which Ockham's argument depends, and the conception of *cause* which he assumes, bear both striking resemblances to and notable differences from similar arguments in modern thought.

I shall now remark on Ockham's notion of *cause*. And since our interest is in efficient causation, we can, without serious loss of generality, restrict ourselves to the efficient cause. Ockham makes it clear that an efficient cause is both a *sine qua non* and a sufficient condition[8] of a given event.[9] Natural (i.e., non-free) causes, however,

7. *Ordinatio*, Prol. q. 9, in *Opera Theologica*, I, 241.
8. *Ordinatio*, dist. 45, q. unica, D: "Istud sufficit ad hoc, quod aliquid sit causa immediata, scilicet quod illa re absoluta posita, ponatur effectus, et ipsa non posita, aliis omnibus concurrentibus quantum ad omnes conditiones et dispositiones consimiles, non ponitur effectus. Unde omne, quod est tale respectu alicuius, est causa immediata illius. . . . Quod autem hoc sufficiat ad hoc, quod aliquid sit causa immediata alterius, videtur esse manifestum, quia si non perit omnis via ad cognoscendum aliquid esse causam alterius immediatam." Cf. *Reportatio*, II, q. 5, K; *Summulae in Libros Physicorum*, II, ch. 3.
9. I say "a given event" rather than "a given *type* of event" deliberately. For Ockham, causal connection is not simply invariable succession. (*Ordinatio*, dist. 2, q. 4, in *Opera Theologica*, II, 145: "Agens naturale in agendo intendit veram rem singularem, quia illud intendit quod per se et primo producitur, sed res singularis per se et primo producitur, igitur etc.") First, the efficacy of causes is no less a part of Ockham's thought than of the thought of other scholastics before and during the fourteenth century. Michalski ("La Physique nouvelle et les differents courants philosophiques au XIV[e] siecle," *Bulletin international de l'Academie polonaise des sciences et des lettres*, Classe de philologie, d'histoire et de philosophie, Annee 1927 [Krakow, 1928], p. 159) quotes a statement from John of Mirecourt which suggests that some, at least, believed in the possibility that action is a mere relation: "Alia opinio posset esse et forte, si liceret eam ponere, multum probabilis, quae poneret, quod actio

always behave as they sometimes behave. This means (a) that a given natural agent always produces the same effect in any patient of a given species. Now since a cause is both *sine qua non* and sufficient, it would appear as if no plurality of cause is allowed. But Ockham, following Aristotle in this consideration, allows that in one sense there is, and in another sense there is not, a plurality of causes.[10]

We must first distinguish between a substance's possession of a property which *is* itself a causal characteristic, and a substance's possession of a property which *has* a causal characteristic. In the second place we distinguish between those causal characteristics which belong to a genus and those which belong to a species. These two distinctions will then give us the following classification of causal characteristics:

A.   In an *infima* species:
     1. All Sj is P
        or
     2. All Sj is P and all P is P
B.   In a genus:
     1. All Gi is P
        or
     2. All Gi is Q and all Q is P

Now Ockham makes the following assumption. If effects of a given kind result from an individual of a given species and from another individual of that same species, then the causes of the effects in question are the same within that species. Thus, whether P results directly from Sj or indirectly, P belongs to every member of Sj in exactly the same way. It could, conceivably, be otherwise. For example, if one member of Sj has Q_1 and another Q_2, it is conceivable that there are two true generalizations: all Q_1 is P, and all Q_2

nihil est: nec motus, nec intentio, sed sunt modi se habendi rerum." But this is, I think, extremely rare. Even Nicolaus of Autrecourt appears to believe in the *efficacy* of causes. Second, Ockham believed in the efficacy of the free will.

10. See Aristotle, *Posterior Analytics*, ii, 17-18, and Sir David Ross's *Commentary on Aristotle's Prior and Posterior Analytics* (Oxford, 1950), pp. 688-72. Ockham's discussion is in *Ordinatio*, Prol., q. 2, art. 2 (*Opera Theologica*, I, 87-96), and in *Summa Logicae*, III, pt. 2, ch. 10. One example given by Ockham of plurality of causes is the production of heat by fire and by the sun's rays. This, evidently, was a source of puzzlement for the scholastics.

is *P*. This is what Ockham denies. It is in this sense that there is no plurality of causes. On the other hand, it is perfectly possible that all *Sj* is *P* and all *Sk* is *P*, where *Sj* ≠ *Sk*. The causal characteristic is thus not "commensurate" with the single species. It is in this sense that there is a plurality of causes. But, since a cause is both *sine qua non* and sufficient, I think that Ockham supposes that there is some common predicate which is convertible with *P* and which is predictable of all species which have *P*. If this is the case, the plurality of causes is only apparent.

I shall now present Ockham's own words, and then comment upon them.

> Suppose it be posited that this is a first principle: 'Every herb of such a species is helpful to a feverish person'. Now this cannot be syllogised from any better-known propositions, but the knowledge of it is taken from an intuitive notice and perhaps from many such intuitive notices. For, because someone sees that health follows in a feverish person after the eating of such an herb and has removed all other causes of health of that feverish person, he evidently knows that this herb was the cause of health and then he has an experience about a single being. It is, however, known to him that all individuals of the same nature have in the affected individual an effect of the same kind if the cases are equally disposed. Hence he accepts with evidence as if a principle: 'every such herb helps the feverish'. . . .
>
> Thus if, by virtue of an intuitive notice, the evident notice is taken of this contingent truth: 'the herb cures such an infirmity', this is a mediate partial cause of the notice of this demonstrable conclusion: 'every such herb cures'. But intuitive notice is only a partial cause, since this notice suffices only if it is evidently known that all individuals of the same kind are both to have effects of the same kind in an affected thing of a given kind and in similar disposition. . . .
>
> Now neither 'every such herb is curative of such an infirmity' nor 'this herb is curative of such an infirmity' is a first proposition derived from experience unless the substance itself were the reason for producing such health. For if some

11. This, as I understand it, is what Aristotle holds.

quality existing in the herbs is the principle of curing, then the proposition in which 'curative' is predicated of whatever has that quality will be a first principle and 'every such herb is curative' will be a demonstrable conclusion. . . .[12]

But still this is a valid consequence: 'This herb is curative, hence, every such herb is curative'. The consequent thus inferred is a conclusion rather than a principle. For the consequence holds by means of the following: 'Whatever thing or property consequent thereupon is true of a given individual can likewise be true of every individual of the same kind'. Thus, from the very fact that this herb has a quality which is a principle of curing a given infirmity, any such herb can have such a quality. . . .

If, however, [we are concerned with] something common to many species, then many experiences are required since an experience is needed for an individual of each of these species. Thus for knowing with evidence that every act is generative of a habit, an experience is needed that an act of a previous is generative of a habit, than an act of a conclusion is generative of a habit, and so of other species. This is true when such a principle is taken precisely from experience [since it it were taken from reasoning such an investigation of each species would not be required]. And under these circumstances, such a deduction does not hold by means of the proposition that 'causes of the same genus are effective of effects of the same genus', . . . or by means of some similar proposition, e.g., that 'whatever is true of something of a given genus can be true of another thing of that same genus'. . . . But the deduction will hold by means of this: 'Whenever something is true of each species of a genus it is true universally of that genus'. And then such a principle about a genus or about something common to many things of diverse kinds is obtained by experience and in some way by induction, namely, by inferring a universal proposition about the genus from all the [pertinent] universals about all the species contained under the genus.[13]

12. I.e., whatever has Q has P; every such herb has Q; every such herb has P. Or, whatever has Q has P; this herb has Q; this herb has P.

13. *Ordinatio*, Prol., q. 2, art. 2 (*Opera Theologica*, I, 87, 90-91, 94-95, 92-93). Cf. Hochstetter, 163-69; Aristotle, *Prior Analytics*, II, ch. 23.

Ockham has given another account[14] of scientific inference which is almost the same as the one I have just presented. The only significant difference is this: in the latter account Ockham expressly admits that even when we are attempting to establish an induction over *infima* species, we sometimes require many experiences:

> It ought also to be noted that frequently, in order to acquire knowledge of the universal proposition, many singulars are required even though the subject of the universal is a species special; for in most cases a singular contingent proposition cannot be evidently known without many apprehensives of single instances, when it is not easy to know that this herb cured a certain invalid and that it was not this doctor who cured him. And so with many other cures, for it is not easy to grasp that which is experienced, because the same effect in species can exist through many causes specifically different.[15]

The explanation of Ockham's reasoning in these passages is very difficult. The problem of establishing *all members of a genus have a given causal characteristic* is easy to solve: it is the well-known complete induction explained in the twenty-third chapter of Book II of Aristotle's *Prior Analytics*. It is the establishment of a causal characteristic of all members of a given species which causes the trouble. In order to explain the difficulties involved I propose first to set forth an argument which I think is absolutely sound, and then to discover whether Ockham's views are interpretable as an argument of this kind.

Suppose we assume (1) that for a given kind of effect E there is a necessary and sufficient condition (from this it follows that there is but one such condition);[16] (2) that there are cases of E which have characteristics exactly as follows:

Case 1 has $P\ A\ B\ C\ E$ Case 3 has $\bar{P}\ A\ B\ C\ \bar{E}$

Case 2 has $P\ F\ G\ H\ E$ Case 4 has $\bar{P}\ F\ G\ H\ \bar{E}$

14. *Summa Logicae*, III, pt. 2, ch. 10.

15. Translated by E. A. Moody, *The Logic of William of Ockham* (London, 1935), p. 241.

16. More exactly, as von Wright points out, that all n. & s. conditions are coextensive, i.e., that they are all n. & s. conditions of one another.

and (3) that these cases are completely known; that is, they are known to have just the characteristics they have in fact.

It is easily seen that A, B, C, F, G, H, or any combination of these single characteristics, are not necessary conditions of E. Hence it follows that none of these characteristics nor any combination of them is sufficient. (For there is, by the assumptions, but one characteristic which is both necessary and sufficient.) Now since, by assumption 1, there is a necessary and sufficient condition of E, it must be P. But this means that all P is E. And therefore, under the specified conditions, it is possible to infer a universal proposition from a certain pair of its instances. Now it is easy to see that this argument fails if any of the assumptions, 1 to 3, is weakened or eliminated. No important universal conclusion can be deduced if, instead of 1, we had required only that there be a sufficient condition for every member of E. For even if we could prove that A, B, C, F, G, H, and combinations are neither necessary nor sufficient, the very best result we could obtain would be that P is a part of a sufficient condition of E. And this is hardly a very informative conclusion. Moreover, if we weaken assumption 2 but retain 1 and 3, we have a complex cause whose degree of complexity cannot be decided by the method proposed above. Again, if we retain 1 and 2 but reject 3, we have the peculiar situation, if the two descriptions are in fact compatible, that although 1 and 2 jointly imply the *truth* of *all P is E* if the two conceptions are *in fact* complete, we cannot *know* that all P is E simply by *knowing* 1 and 2. The doubt will still linger that maybe there is some characteristic other than P which is common to our cases. If that were so, we would have a possibly complex cause to deal with as before. These well-known considerations have been referred to in the literature as the difficulties of a plurality of causes, a complexity of causes, and possible hidden causes.

It is clear that Ockham's procedure does not explicitly follow the pattern of the argument I have presented, for he allows for a "plurality of causes," and he notices the difficulty of eliminating rival candidates for the cause on a given occasion. The problem of elimination is especially acute. Let us see how he would have proceeded.

Suppose we have a possible agent substance, call it X, of species Sj, and a possible patient substance, Y, of species Sk. Also we shall denote the agent quality (if any) by Q and the causal characteristic (if any) by P. Our problem is, first of all, to show that X has P, or that X has Q and Q is P.

Accordingly, we start without X and observe that Y does not suffer the passion corresponding to the action P. Then we introduce X. If, when X_1 approximates Y_1, Y_1 suffers the passion corresponding to P, we can say that, in this case, X_1 has P or has a quality Q which has P. Thus we know that, under given circumstances, Y does not suffer the passion (let us for convenience call it P^1), and that when the only difference is X_1's presence, it does have P^1. We reason as follows: nothing but X_1 was sufficient to produce P^1 in Y_1. Now we do not yet know that X_1 or a quality of X_1 is singly sufficient to produce P^1 in Y_1. For X_1 or Q of X_1 might be only a differential condition. Hence we must now try another experiment. We must either (a) introduce X_1 to Y_1 under entirely different circumstances, or (b) introduce another member of Sj, say X_2, to under different circumstances Y_1, or (c) introduce X_2 to another member of Sk, say Y_2, under different circumstances. But this, again, will not prove that X_2 has P. For again, X_2 may very well be or have only a differential function, i.e., it may be that X_1 alone is not sufficient but only a contributing condition. Ockham's argument does not seem, therefore, to establish what he claims for it.

However, there is a chance that his distinction between a passion which depends directly on the substantial form of the agent and one which is a quality of the agent but not deducible from the substantial nature, and his distinction between a property which belongs primarily to an agent and a property which belongs only secondarily to an agent, will help. Let us recall that we have the following possibilities:

Sj is P or Sj is Q and Q is P

Gi is P or Gi is Q and Q is P

Ockham, it seems, assumes either that sooner or later we shall come to a primary property of some genus which will be convertible with that genus, or that but one species[17] of a genus will have a given

17. It need not, of course, be an infima species.

property and will then be convertible with that property.[18] This, if correct, would provide us with a theoretical system in which the conditions of the argument could be fulfilled. For we could then eliminate the possible plurality of causes.

But there are two fatal objections to this procedure. First of all, we cannot apply it even under the most ideal assumption of completely known instances. And, in the second place, it is a wholly arbitrary assumption that either exactly one species of a single natural genus or all the species of a single natural genus have a given characteristic. Hence the genus of things possessing a given causal characteristic will be an artificial genus, namely the species which just happen to have the causal characteristic in question.

The last-mentioned result is entirely out of keeping with Ockham's conception. For a causal characteristic, even though it is neither deducible from the essence of the genus nor immediately discernible as entailed by that essence, is the discursive expression of a causal efficacy of each of the members of a kind. To a wholly artificial kind the application of the rule *Whatever is true of each species of a genus is universally true of the genus* is a purely nominal or verbal affair.

I conclude, with some reluctance, that Ockham's account of the methods of empirical science is on his own terms inadequate. Now, he is not to be too severely censured for this. He inherited from Aristotle an account of science which was almost entirely deductive.[19] Aristotle recognized that the ultimate premises of the special sciences must be established by some process other than deduction. But his account of this process is, as Bonitz once observed, extremely obscure, and the demands he put upon these ultimate premises, certainty, necessity, etc., could not possibly be met. Ockham attempted to meet these demands while at the same time he realized clearly that any insight into the relation between an agent and its powers was out of the question. That is to say, he realized the radically empirical origin of all our natural knowledge. Yet he supposed that the acquaintance with single events together with some general maxims

18. At any rate, Aristotle, *Posterior Analytics*, 98^b 25-35, definitely holds this.

19. Cf. *Posterior Analytics*, II, 19, 99^{b}15-100^{b}17; *Metaphysics*, A, 980^{b}25-981^{a}12.

about the regular behavior of non-free agents would yield indubitably true universal propositions. That he failed in this attempt is hardly an occasion for wonderment. His statement of the method of science as he saw it has two merits. The first is that it is, despite the obscurities I have dwelt upon, far clearer than that of Aristotle or those of his commentators with whose works I am acquainted. The second is that the limitations of Aristotelian empiricism as well as the advantages become evident in Ockham's discussion, even though he, in all likelihood, was unaware of the limitations.

4

The Problem
of Sensory Cognition

It has often been suggested that the problems connected with the possibility, nature, and extent of human knowledge were introduced into philosophy by Descartes and by those who were influenced by him. Thomas Reid found that the principal error of the British Empiricists consists in the "ideal system" of Descartes.[1] But, according to Reid, "The vulgar know nothing about this idea; it is a creature of philosophy, introduced to account for and explain the manner of our perceiving external objects."[2] Thus the main source of scepticism is the interposition of "ideas" between our consciousness and the objects of awareness. That this view of the matter is, at least, *simpliste* requires no great argument. The work which must be done to achieve a more just view is hardly indicated by such oversimplification. Moreover, the revival and development of the philosophy of common sense since Henry Sidgwick and G. E. Moore has further obscured some of the important historical facts about the problem of knowledge. I propose here to indicate something of the

First printed in Edward D. Simmons, ed., *Essays on Knowledge and Methodology* (Ken Cook Company Publishers: Milwaukee, 1965). Reprinted by permission.

1. Sir William Hamilton, ed., *The Works of Thomas Reid, D.D..*, 2 vols. (Edinburgh: Maclachlan, Stewart and Co., 1846), I, 103.

2. Ibid., p. 293.

pre-Cartesian development of these problems in order to show that
the issues which have concerned philosophy since Descartes were discussed in ancient and medieval thought.

It would not be difficult to show that some of the issues are
already present in pre-Platonic philosophy. One precious fragment
from Democritus, whatever its original meaning, was read in antiquity
as meaning that infrasensible and sensible realities are to be distinguished. And, from another quarter, the relativism of Protagoras provided further reasons for distinguishing between what is directly
accessible to sensation and what perhaps must be obtained by other
than the sensitive capacities. It was, however, Plato above all who
introduced into Western thought the suggestion that sensation results
from the action of outer objects on the percipient organism and that
the object becomes present to consciousness by a phantasm. This
already contains the kernel of the idea that something intervenes between the knower and the object known. Whatever may be the ultimate exegesis of Aristotelian views on the subject, the notion that
"sensation is the reception of the form of sensible objects without
the matter" ("*αἴσθησίς ἐστι τὸ δεκτικὸν τῶν αἰσθητῶν εἰδῶν
ἄνευ τῆς ὕλης*")[3] and that "objects do not come to exist in the soul
but only the forms of objects" ("*οὐ γὰρ ὁ λίθος ἐν τῇ ψυχῇ, ἀλλὰ τὸ
εἶδος*")[4] easily lead to the doctrine that we know objects by knowing the intermediaries they produce in our senses and consciousness,
even though a well-known exegesis of this doctrine states that a species is "id quo aliquid intelligitur" rather than "id quod intelligitur."[5]

The Stoic doctrine of the *presentation* (*φαντασία*) as an imprint
on the soul (*τύπωσιν ἐν φυχῇ*)[6] leaves little doubt that the presentation is an intermediary between the cognizing agent and its object;
the genuine presentation "is one which proceeds from a real object,
agrees with that object itself, ·and has been imprinted seal-fashion
and stamped on the mind"[7] and it is reasonably clear that here we
have something distinct from the external object by means of which
the object is known. The Sceptics' critique of this notion reveals that
the so-called kataleptic phantasy is, at best, an effect of an object,

3. *De Anima,* ii, 12, 424ª18.
4. Ibid., iii, 8, 431ᵇ30.
5. Thomas Aquinas, *Summa Theologiae,* Part I, q. 85, a. 2.
6. Diogenes Laertius, *Vitae Philosophorum,* vii, 45–56. Cf. Aristotle, *De
Anima,* ii, 12, 424ª19-20.
7. Diogenes Laertius, *Vitae Philosophorum,* vii, 46.

and, indeed, one that cannot be trusted, because similar impressions not thus caused can also be present to consciousness in such a way that we cannot discriminate between the genuine and the bogus.

In Epicurean epistemology, the point we wish to make is, if anything, clearer than in the case of the Stoics. Epicurus explicitly states that "it is by the entrance of something from external objects that we see their shapes and think of them. For external things would not stamp on us their own nature of color and form through the medium of the air which is between them and us or by means of rays of light or currents of any sort going from us to them,[8] so well as by the entrance into our eyes or minds, . . . of certain films coming from the things themselves, these films or outlines being of the same color and shape as the external things themselves."[9]

In modern thought the introduction of sense data or sensibilia as intermediaries between cognitions and their objects, insofar as it depends on Descartes and Locke, differs from the medieval assumption of such intermediaries in a number of important respects. The theory of Locke is explicitly causal: the data of exterior sensation are "ideas" which are caused by outer objects. The only immediate objects of consciousness are ideas, and strictly, our knowledge of or belief in external objects should be inferential. Neither these objects nor their qualities are directly perceived. In the case of Descartes, some of the qualities which objects seem to have are actually affections of the soul. If N. K. Smith is correct, Descartes holds that the physical patterns in the pineal gland are directly inspected, but they, too, are representatives, albeit physical representatives, of the objects which comprise the physical world outside of the body. Medieval views cannot be easily summarized, but the ones most familiar to us are (1) the doctrine of sensible and intelligible species, and (2) the doctrine of *esse apparens*. Some of the issues involved in the explanation of perceptual consciousness are illustrated by the controversy between Petrus Aureoli and William Ockham concerning whether it

8. This is a reference to the Platonic theory of vision as extromission of rays from the eyes.

9. Diogenes Laertius, *Vitae Philosophorum*, x, 49. Though much of this is Democritean, the emphasis that the films have the same shapes and colors as the objects from which they came is Epicurus' attempt to avoid the sceptical consequences of Democritus' decoloration of the physical objects. See Cyril Bailey, *Greek Atomists and Epicurus* (Oxford: Clarendon Press, 1928).

is necessary to postulate the appearing or intentional being of an object in consciousness. I shall begin by stating the views and some of the main arguments of Aureoli on this subject and then present Ockham's objections together with some objections of John of Mirecourt (who, on this subject, generally follows Ockham). Not the least of interesting aspects is the fact that the points, the arguments, and the very examples on both sides of this medieval debate are duplicated in recent and contemporary discussions in twentieth-century British and American philosophy.

Petrus Aureoli (d. 1322) composed his *Scriptum super Primum Sententiarum* in the second decade of the fourteenth century. In it he argued, "In the act of the intellect it is necessarily the case that the thing which is understood is posited in a certain intentional, conspicuous, and apparent being."[10] In the cognition of an object that is actually present to the percipient, the object itself as existing for thought takes on an intentional being in consciousness;[11] this is brought about by the intellect assimilating itself to the thing.

However, the *Doctor Facundus* holds that intuitive cognition can exist without the present existence of an external object; and, because in intuitive cognition an object is cognized as present whether or not it is present or even exists, it is possible for intentional being to have no corresponding object external to the mind of the cognizing agent.

10. Q. 14, a. 1, dist. 3, in *Scriptum super Primum Sententiarum*, ed. E. Buytaert, O.F.M., 2 vols. (St. Bonaventure, N.Y.: Franciscan Institute, 1953 and 1956), II, 696: "Prima quidem quod in actu intellectus de necessitate res intellecta ponitur in quodam esse intentionali conspicuo et apparenti." Cf. ibid., I, 37, q. 25, a. 1, dist. 9: "Quod in omni intellectione necesse est quod res ponatur in esse intentionali, et illa est apparitio obiectiva seu forma specularis."

11. Q. 25, a. 1, dist. 9, in *Scriptum super Primum Sententiarum*, 2 vols. (Rome, 1596 and 1605), I, 320: "Omnis intellectio exigit rem positam in esse intentionali, et illa est forma specularis, de qua isti loquuntur, sed deficiunt a veritate in tribus. . . . Tertio, quia credunt quod per illum procedat intellectus ad res, cum illa sit vera res quam intellectus speculator. . . . Unde patet quomodo res ipsa conspiciuntur mente, et illud, quod intuemur, non est forma alia specularis, sed ipsamet res habens esse apparens, et hoc est mentis conceptus sive notitia obiectiva."

The proof that there must be an intentional being present to consciousness begins by appealing to "many experiences."[12] The *Doctor Facundus* assures us that this appeal to experience takes precedence over any arguments, since experience is the foundation of science and art. If he can prove that apparent being must be assumed in sensation, it must also be assumed in intellection, because the intellect is more capable of activity than the senses and this apparent being in sensation is due, in part, to the activity of the senses.

The first experience is as follows. When a person is carried in a boat on a river, the trees and the bank sometimes appear to be moved. Now, this motion cannot be attributed to the vision itself. If it were, we should have to say that sight is a reflexive power, since in this case sight would sense itself. But it cannot be supposed that the motion in question is in the trees, for in this assumption the trees would really be moved. Hence the motion exists intentionally, or in perceived existence.

The second experience. When an ignited stick is rapidly moved in a circular manner, a circle appears in the air to the observer. This circle might be supposed to be in the stick, in the air, or in the vision itself. None of these hypotheses will do, so that again we seem forced to conclude that the circle exists merely in intentional being.

The third experience concerns the half-submerged stick which appears to be broken, and the fifth concerns the multitude of colors on the neck of a pigeon. Aureoli says little about this, but it is clear that we are to conclude that the fractionation of the stick and the colors exist only in intentional or apparent being.

The fourth experience is one which has been often used both before Aureoli[13] and after. When we press against one eye, two candles appear where before there was but one. Hence, there are two in apparent being, although only one in real being.

The sixth experience is derived from the variety of mirror images and is explicitly derived from Al-Hazan's *Perspective*, Books IV, V,

12. Q. 14, a. 1, dist. 3, in *Scriptum*, the Buytaert ed., II, 696 ff. Cf. Prooemium, q. 2, in I, 198 ff.

13. For example, by Augustine, *De Trinitate*, xi, chap. 4.

and VI (Aureoli acknowledges this as the source of his information). Here Aureoli alludes to the various virtual images which are produced with concave and convex mirrors. These virtual images appear sometimes to be behind the mirror, sometimes between the mirror and the observer.[14] The virtual image cannot be a "real species" because, in some cases, the image appears larger than the mirror (but no accident exceeds its subject). In other cases, the image appears to be behind the mirror at a distance which exceeds the thickness of the mirror. These images cannot be real existences, nor can they be supposed to be something existing in the eye. "It remains, therefore, that such an image is only the appearance of a thing having apparent and intentional existence. The thing itself is behind the mirror in perceived, judged, and apparent existence."[15]

The seventh and eighth experiences are taken from St. Augustine, *De Trinitate*, Book xi, chapter 4. A person who gazes steadily at the sun and afterward turns away will see bright spots (*rotunditates*) before him which soon vanish. People who gaze at something red or look for some time through lattices and afterward look at letters in a book will see them as red or latticed. "There is no doubt in these cases that the lattice-work or the redness has only apparent or intentional being."[16]

Aureoli concludes this discussion by saying that those who deny that many things have merely intentional and apparent existences and who think that all the things which are seen exist *in rerum natura* deny that there are any deceptions, and, consequently, fall into the Protagorean error of believing that whatever appears exists.

Having, to his own satisfaction, shown that the exterior senses by their activity produce apparent or intentional being, Aureoli argues to the same effect for imagination. When I think of my father, for example, he is posited in intentional being. If interior and exterior senses produce intentional being, the intellect *a fortiori* does so as well.

14. See Philotheus Boehner, O.F.M., ed., "Aureoli–Appendix: Commentarius in I[m] Sententiarum, Prologi q. 1," *Franciscan Studies*, 8 (1948), 411–16. See p. 413.

15. Q. 14, a. 1, dist. 3, in *Scriptum*, Buytaert ed., II, 697: "Relinquitur igitur quod sit sola apparentia rei vel res habens esse apparens et intentionale, ita ut ipsamet res sit infra speculum in esse viso iudicato et apparenti."

16. Ibid.: ". . . quae quidem cancellatura vel rubedo non dubium quod non habent nisi esse intentionale et apparens."

In defending his points, Aureoli anticipates the main objection that his critics will exploit against him. "But perhaps it will be said against these experiences, firstly that they are false, deceptive, and erroneous visions, and that we ought not to argue from such errors and deceptions to true visions; secondly, that they are not visions at all but only the judgment of the *sensus communis*, by which we merely suppose that we see (as is made plain in *De Anima*, ii). Thus, such deceived persons do not really see but they only seem to see because the *sensus communis* judges so. But these evasions do not refute the foregoing demonstration. The first argument rather confirms than evades the conclusion we have drawn, because no act exists in the visual potency which does not participate in the specific nature of vision. Both Augustine and Averroes expressly say this: Augustine, for his part, concludes 'That *was* a vision,' and the Commentator says that 'Man senses such things by the five senses.' ... The second evasion does not succeed, partly because it denies what Averoes and Augustine say . . . , partly because the common sense is never actualized unless the particular senses are themselves actualized as *De Anima*, ii, makes plain; partly because, if the common sense judges that the eye sees, it is necessary that there is something in the eye, namely the appearance of a thing."[17]

Aureoli uses these experiences along with others—specifically the experiences of those who are dreaming, those who are stricken by fear or illness, the experiences of people with weak eyes, and the experiences of people who are deceived, by magicians, for example—to show that intuitive cognition can occur without the actual presence of objects. To the same purpose, he appeals to the theological principle, so often invoked in the fourteenth century, that God can accomplish anything which does not imply a contradiction. Now, since any intuitive notice is something absolute which founds a relation to a thing known intuitively, God can conserve such an absolute intuition even if the relation and the thing are corrupted.

There are at least two known critiques of this doctrine mentioned by Michalski:[18] that of William of Ockham in his *Questions on the*

17. Prooemium, q. 2, in *Scriptum*, Buytaert ed., I, 200–201.
18. K. Michalski, "Le Criticisme de la scepticisme dans la philosophie du XIVe siecle," *Bulletin international de l'Academie polonaise des sciences et des lettres*, Classe d'histoire et de philosophie, Annee 1925 (Cracow, 1926), pp. 41-122. See esp. pp. 96-112.

Sentences[19] and that of John of Mirecourt.[20] The latter seems to me to depend considerably on the former. Ockham's critique is introduced by a careful restatement of all of Aureoli's arguments, usually quoted *au pied de la lettre*. Then Ockham states that "since I have seen little of the works of this Doctor [sc. Aureoli], indeed, if all the times I have examined his statements were put together they would fill out the space of but one day, I do not wish to argue against him at length. For I might be able to argue with some levity, from ignorance of his statements, rather against his words than his intention. But as the conclusion, as far as it sounds, seems to me false, I shall argue against it, whether or not my arguments succeed in refuting his intentions."[21]

We must not be put off by this disclaimer, for actually Ockham devotes much effort to the refutation of the doctrine of Aureoli.

Ockham's first argument: Either this apparent and intentional being exists objectively and has no *subjective* existence or it has subjective existence. But the first alternative is excluded, because if it were true, either a true quality would never be apprehended by the senses or two objects would be sensed, the real quality and the objective being. Also, nothing is an object of sensation essentially and properly save a real sensible thing. The second alternative cannot be maintained either, because if something has subjective being it is a real being, so that if the apparent being existed subjectively it would be a real being. Moreover, we cannot say that the objective or apparent being, in veridical cognition, is the same as the thing existing outside the mind. If it were, the objective being would exist without perception, because the real being exists when it is not observed.

A further argument is as follows. When there are two things appearing to some cognitive or sensitive potency, for instance whiteness and intentional whiteness, and there is a need to distinguish one of these from the other, then the reason which obliged us to say that one requires an apparent being can be applied to the apparent being itself. In other words, the apparent being itself, in order to be sensed

19. I, d. 27, 1. 3.

20. "Lectura Primi Libri Sententiarum," q. 4, in *Questioni inedite di Giovanni de Mirecourt sulla cognoscenza*, Rivista critica di storia della filosofia, Anno XIII (Florence, 1958), pp. 415–28.

21. *Ordinatio* [super Primum Sententiarum], dist 27, 1. 3, H.

or cognized, requires another apparent being in turn, and this leads to an infinite regress. If it is maintained that the apparent being requires no medium in order to be sensed or cognized, the same may be said of a real being: no medium between the percipient and the object is required. Hence, the *esse apparens* is posited in vain.

Ockham proceeds to his first general point. In no intuitive notice, whether sensitive or intellective, is there anything constituted as a medium between the external object and the act of knowing. The thing itself is seen or apprehended immediately without any medium between itself and the act. And just as there is no medium between the external object and intuitive cognition, so there is no medium between the object and abstractive cognition.

Whether any objective beings are needed to explain universal concepts is a matter on which Ockham hesitates. He allowed several probable theories on this subject at the time he wrote the *Questions on the Sentences*, one of which is that universals have objective existence, whilst the others require only subjective qualities in the soul.[22] It is noteworthy that in his later writings even this concession to objective beings is removed, and even universal cognitions are explained without recourse to objective beings.

It is incumbent on Ockham to show in detail how the eight "experiences" of Aureoli can be explained without recourse to any objective medium between the knower and the external world. Consequently, he replies to each of these experiences as follows.

To the first experience. The proposition *the trees are moved* does exist objectively in the mind, and it is true that the mind can form such a proposition and assent to, or dissent from, it. But this is nothing to the purpose at hand. If it is said that the proposition *the trees appear to the senses to be moved* is true even for animals lacking cognition, we must say that, if such a statement is so understood as to imply that any movement whatsoever is apprehended by the senses, it is false. For only motion that is, or that can be, real is apprehended by the senses. On the other hand, if the statement

22. See Ockham, *Ordinatio*, dist 2, q. 8. See also Philotheus Boehner, O.F.M., "The Text Tradition of Ockham's 'Ordinatio'," *Collected Articles on Ockham*, ed. E. Buytaert, O.F.M. (St. Bonaventure, N.Y.: Franciscan Institute, 1958), and J. R. Weinberg, "Ockham's Conceptualism," *Philosophical Review*, 50 (1941), 523–28.

means that in sensation there are apprehensions of diverse objects in virtue of which some operations can be elicited from the recipient like the operations which a body actually moved elicits from the sentient, the proposition is true. But it does not follow from this that any motion appears; it only follows that there are, in sensation, many apprehensions equivalent to operations elicited by appearance or vision by which motion appears. Thus no motion is seen in this case. The trees are seen at different distances and aspects because of the motion of the percipient in the boat, and the trees appear to be moved such that the following two propositions are equivalent: (1) The trees are seen successively at different distances and aspects by the eye moved in the motion of the boat without any medium produced in any sort of real or intentional existence; (2) The trees appear to the eye to be moved.

To the second experience. As in reply to the first experience, Ockham maintains that while no circle appears when the burning stick is rapidly moved around in the air, the intellect sometimes believes that *There is a circle in the air* is true. Now no circle can be said to appear to the eye, unless this simply means that there are operations of the mind similar to those which are called forth by the apprehensions of a circle in the genuine case. It no more follows that because a circle is judged to be in the air it is actually there than it follows from *God is judged to be a body* that God is a body.

Similar arguments are adduced against the third and fourth experiences, the stick partly submerged and the double image of the candle. We can explain these cases without recourse to anything but the external objects and the cognitive acts of the cognitive power of the mind.

With respect to the fifth experience, Ockham holds that the colors actually exist on the neck of the piegeon or in the immediately adjacent air.

To the sixth experience, which involves mirror images, Ockham holds that the thing itself is seen in the mirror, that nothing imaginable is required here save the thing which is understood, the mirror, and several other existing things, together with the judgment which exists *subjectively* in the soul, because the thing is not *within* the mirror intentionally or actually. In this way, if sense could have a judgment distinct from sensation, it could judge that the thing is in the mirror without any medium. It might be argued that because the very same thing is now judged to exist within the mirror and *previously* was not, it has a *judged* being which it did not previously have and it has an intentional being which it did not have. But to this Ockham replies that a thing is now judged to be within the mirror not because something other than the thing occurs but because the judgment now exists in the cognitive power and previously did not. Hence the thing which is not really within the mirror is judged to be there without any medium.

John of Mirecourt has a question[23] concerning whether in the cognition of a thing (existing or not existing) some entity is caused in the thing, the medium, or the organ other than the act of *habitus* in the cognitive power. Of the six principal conclusions in this question, I am interested here only in the first one directed against Aureoli. It is worth noticing, however, that conclusions 4, 5, and 6 are concerned with the doctrine of *species*, and this shows, I believe, that Mirecourt (as well as Ockham) rejected the species doctrine along with Aureoli's theory of intentional being on similar grounds.

The general question is answered in the negative by an appeal to the principle of economy. Nothing is to be assumed or required for any effect unless one of the following grounds can be invoked: (1) an argument which follows logically from self-evident premises, or at least follows logically from propositions more probable than their opposites; (2) authority which may not be rejected; (3) experience. Now the theory that cognition produces an entity distinct from the cognitive act or *habitus* cannot invoke any of these necessities.

John of Mirecourt presents the "experiences" of Aureoli in detail but not always with Ockham's exact fidelity. His replies to each of these experiences follow Ockham's general line, but it is worth something to go through these replies, if only to make clear that both Mirecourt and Ockham attempt to explain all the phenomena as errors of judgment.

He begins with a very general observation and then deals with the experiences specifically:

1. A thing can be so applied to sight or the sight can be so disposed that a man in virtue of such a vision can, unless he is otherwise

23. See note 20.

corrected, have many erroneous judgments; for example, he will judge that he sees what he does not see and what he sees he will judge he does not see, and can be thus deceived in many ways.

2. A person carried in a boat through the water does not see trees moved, but he has successively one vision and then another by which he sees continuously trees in one position and another by reason of the movement of the boat, and in virtue of this, unless he is otherwise corrected, he judges that the trees are moved.

3. Such a person does not see the motion of trees nor does he see any motion, because there is no motion in the trees nor in anything seen by him in this case, although he himself is moved *per accidens* in the motion of the boat.

4. When an ignited stick is moved in the air in a circular manner, no colored circle terminated in the air or in the stick is seen, although it appears that there is a circle in the air by a false and erroneous judgment.

5. No such circle is seen there or appears to be there, though it is judged in virtue of vision that there is such a circle there, unless the observer is otherwise corrected. The reason for this is that sight follows the stick moved in a circular way, and because of the rapidity of the stick's movement a man does not know whether diverse parts of one circle succeed each other or whether it is moved in a circular way.

6. The person seeing a stick one part of which is in water and the other part out of water does not see a broken stick nor any breakage in the stick, though he judges that he sees such a thing. The reason is the diversity of the media through which diverse parts of the stick are revealed.

7. A person viewing one candle when one eye is pressed upward does not in this case see two candles, although it seems to him that he sees two candles unless his understanding is otherwise rectified. The reason for this is that, according to St. Augustine,[24] the concourse of aspects is impeded by reason of the lifting of the eye, whence as Augustine himself states, if a man had but one eye he would never judge this when the eye was lifted.

24. *De Trinitate,* xi, ch. 2, no. 4. "Ex uno quippe oculo quolibet modo deducto, aut impresso, aut intorto, si alter clauses est, dupliciter videri aliquid quod sit unum nullo pacto potest."

8. In the neck of the pigeon there are not diverse colors, though because of the different showings, just as happens in a piece of cloth because of the greater and lesser inclusion of light and diverse parts of the cloth or the neck, a man judges that there are various colors there. This is clear because if such a cloth of uniform surface were presented, a man would only judge unity of color.

9. If a person views a mirror (unless otherwise corrected), he judges the image of a thing to be in the mirror, although there is none there, but he sees the thing by a reflex line and he judges the species of that thing to be in the mirror. The entire cause of this is that he sees a thing by a reflex line.

10. He who sees the sun for some time does not see any circle in the air, though by an erroneous judgment he judges that he sees such. And the cause is a strong imagination remaining and the impression of light in the eye.

11. He who sees red or a lattice for some time, if afterwards he looks at letters, does not see any redness unless the letters *are* red, nor does he see any latticework, although he judges that he sees such. The cause is strong imagination.

12. In deception, a man only sees things which are there. None of these things acquires any additional being or any entity by virtue of vision, although the deceived person judges that he sees something which he does not see. The reason is either the opposition of mirrors by the magic art, or the indisposition of the medium, or the indisposition of the organ.

The main objection which Ockham and Mirecourt develop against the *esse intentionale* of Aureoli is that it is a superfluous element of theory. It is not needed to explain the facts of sensitive or cognitive consciousness. Their main substitute for the *esse intentionale* is judgment, and, in the cases cited, erroneous judgment. Ockham develops this theme by explaining that, in these special cases, external stimuli set up operations in the mind similar to those which are involved in the normal cases.

Ockham and Mirecourt extended their condemnation of *esse intentionale* to cover all postulation of any entities other than the sensing or cognizing subject and object. This included the sensible and intelligible *species*. According to Ockham, species are not necessary nor would they suffice to explain sensation or cognition.[25] He was so opposed to anything of this sort that in his latest philosophical writings he rejected *objective being* even as an explanation of conceptual thinking. This theory is rejected on the grounds of economy, because such an objective being would impede the cognition of a thing, because God could make a common concept without such an objective being, because such a thing is difficult or impossible to imagine since it is neither substance nor accident, and because such an objective being differs more from real things than any real thing differs from any other.

In this dispute between Aureoli and his critic there is obviously some right on both sides. There is, I think, no possibility of explaining away the existence of qualitatively identifiable features of the visual field which are assignable to no external objects in virtual imagery, hallucinating experiences, etc. The insistence that in these cases there is *always* a notable difference from the perceptions of things in the physical world is really of no avail. For as these experiences are sometimes very fleeting, it is impossible to say how much of what we later suppose we witnessed was part of the constellation of qualities in our visual field and how much was supplemented in various ways by habitual association, etc. As a consequence, those who, like Austin, hold that we didn't properly "size up what we saw" are really avoiding the important issue, namely, whether there were some items presented which we mistook for a familiar object but which, in fact, were totally disconnected with any such object. On the other hand, some illusory perceptual situations can very well be explained in terms of misjudgment, though I very much doubt whether *misjudgment* is the best term to use here, for it seems to me that in these cases the data of sentience are supplemented by habitual expectation and the like, so that the situation is more complex than the term *misjudgment* suggests.

Also, what does or may appear is quite plainly misdescribed by the proponents of the *esse intentionale*. In my opinion, at least, the terms used to describe or denote the contents of awareness when we are not in fact witnessing real objects or events are equivocal. A larger vocabulary would avoid much of the trouble here. Thus, instead of saying that I see a flowerpot in a place where there is no

25. *Reportatio* [super Secundum Sententiarum], 1. 15, O.

flowerpot, as in the case of the virtual image produced by the concave mirror, when I am not deluded the proper language would be "I see such and such a shape, color, etc., so-and-so deployed." Of course, if I am deluded, the proper language to use is "I see a flowerpot there." In this case, we must not say "I really saw nothing" but rather "I saw something but it was not a physical object."

It is clear from this debate between Aureoli and his critics that the doctrine that something intervenes between objects and percipients antedates Descartes and the seventeenth-century doctrines of primary and secondary qualities. No revolution in science was required, therefore, to cause men to be puzzled about the explanation of sensory cognition in the face of perceptually deceptive situations.

The reader of any of the British Realists of the past sixty years does not have to be told that the doctrine of Peter Aureoli has many affinities with the doctrine which postulates sense data in order to account for veridical and deceptive perception of external objects. If he has read the criticism of this doctrine by Ryle, Austin, and others, he will see how closely these criticisms parallel those of Ockham and Mirecourt. There are, undoubtedly, important differences which we may not overlook. The most important of these is emphasis on the language used to describe aberrant or abnormal perceptional situations. H. H. Price has summarized their view in this way:

1. The normal perceptual situation is primary. Illusion, hallucination, and the like can only be understood in terms of normal perception. Conceptually, the illusory situations are parasitic on the normal cases.

2. Perceptual verbs are used as verbs of accomplishment. It is incorrect to say that we ever see that which does not exist.

We may add to this the further doctrine that the sense-datum language is parasitic in the language of physical objects.

I do not wish to go into these contentions in detail at this time. There are so many issues involved that each of them would require a separate essay. I shall, therefore, restrict myself to some very brief comments:

1. It seems clear to me that we could learn a language only by coordinating word sounds or other potential symbols with "objects" having sufficient permanence to be available for repeated reference.

From this fact, nothing can be inferred about the ultimate constitution of the world or about the primary data of perceptual consciousness. If there are compelling reasons to understand the "permanent objects" as constellations or series of momentary particulars, this can be made consistent with the fact that our perceptions and our language are primarily related to the constellations as wholes rather than to their constituents. Hence it seems clear that the nature of learning a language does not automatically determine anything about the ultimate nature of things. We should not permit an ineluctable human infirmity to decide what is the structure of the world. The relevance of this to the present discussion is this. It is easier to adopt a sense-datum theory, as Price has indicated, if we are not initially committed to a substance ontology. Arguments that language commits us to such an ontology seem to me inconclusive.

It is not clear to me that, because we could not speak of delusive perceptual situations unless we recognize the normal situations, we are committed to any view about the abnormal cases; and, in particular, the explanation of the abnormal may very well involve appeal to entities which might not be required to explain the normal case. It is only when we interpret the normal case by a conceptual framework which has no room for anything but substances and their attributes that sense data (in modern terminology) or *esse apparentes* (in Aureoli's language) are automatically excluded.

2. The doctrine that perceptual verbs are accomplishment words does not settle the matter even if the doctrine is correct. For there are perfectly correct senses of *see, notice,* etc. applicable in cases where no physical objects or events external to the organisms are involved.

BIBLIOGRAPHY

Boehner, Philotheus, O.F.M. "Notitia Intuitiva of Non-Existents According to Peter Aureoli, O.F.M. (1322)," *Franciscan Studies*, 8 (1948), 388–416.
Gilson, Etienne. *History of Christian Philosophy in the Middle Ages*. New York: Random House, 1955.

Michalski, K. "Le Criticisme de la scepticisme dans la philosophie du XIVe siecle," *Bulletin international de l'Academie polonaise des lettres*. Classe d'histoire et de philosophie, Annee 1925. Cracow, 1926. Pp. 41–122.

Prezioso, F. "La Teoria dell'essere apparente nella gnoselogia di Pietro Aureolo," *Studi francescani*, 22 (1950), 15–43.

5

Fourteenth- and Twentieth-Century Positivism

The subject of this symposium is somewhat curious because it is patently clear that the motives of the fourteenth-century philosopher-theologians were radically different from those of the positivists of the twentieth century. The problems of two such widely separated periods are certainly bound to be different. The limitations of thought within a clearly defined set of theological commitments and the predominant theological concerns of the fourteenth century are characteristic of that age; the concern to rid natural science of metaphysics by the logical clarification of thought is a principal feature of twentieth-century positivism. This is only the beginning of our troubles. The larger question that is posed by our topic is whether there are any perennial problems which thinkers of different times and climates of opinion can fairly be supposed to have considered and answered in recognizably similar ways. Then there is the further difficulty of attempting to characterize an age about which we know as yet very little. Some works of some of the outstanding authors of the fourteenth century have been edited (though few have been translated) during the fifteenth, sixteenth, and seventeenth centuries, and some more recently. But the researches of Michalski and others

Paper read at the Western Division Meetings of the American Philosophical Association, May 5, 1960.

suggest the wealth of materials in manuscripts which would take easily a century to transcribe and edit in modern editions. And until we know much more about these as yet unedited materials it is foolish to attempt any generalizations beyond the very obvious ones I have already suggested. All that we can do at present is to examine some doctrines of a few authors of the fourteenth century in the hope that they will give us some basis of comparison.

We must begin by suggesting the possibility that authors of such widely separated periods were bothered by somewhat similar problems, and that sometimes they provided comparable solutions to such problems. It is hard to justify such an assumption, but when you begin to consider the matter, even harder to deny it absolutely. For an absolute denial amounts to saying that neither metaphysics nor epistemology nor even logic itself has any genuine history: unless we suppose that there is some resemblance between some basic issues in philosophy as it was pursued in past ages and at present, no basis for interpretation or criticism remains. This is not to deny that new discoveries, in logic, for instance, throw an entirely new light on old problems, nor is it to deny that progress is possible. On the contrary, a presupposition of progress in intellectual matters is precisely the similarity of the issues and the continuity of procedures that can be used to make them.

I will begin with some of the philosophical work of Nicolas of Autrecourt and compare it with doctrines which we associate with modern, and more specifically with recent, positivistic thought.

The first thing worthy of comment is the relatively advanced state of logical theory in the fourteenth century. The Syllogistic of Aristotle was only a part of the logic manuals and treatises of the Middle Ages. In addition, there were chapters on what we nowadays call semantics, the logic of propositions, the so-called insolubles, and so on. The chief importance of this development was, as I think, an understanding of the nature of logical inference which was not again achieved until comparatively recent times. Indeed, one of the central tenets of Autrecourt depends on this clarity about the nature of inference and of logical truth. I do not want to suggest that Autrecourt discovered any of these features of logical inference. As I shall indicate, they are implicit in some of Aristotle's statements, some of the Megarian and Stoic logicians added more, and the differences between logically necessary and logically contingent statements began to emerge quite clearly in the logical treatises of the twelfth century (for example, Abelard). Again, the decisive application to metaphysical and epistemological problems was accomplished by Al-Ghazali in the eleventh century (although there is little reason to suppose that he had any direct influence on the authors of the early fourteenth century)[1]. As far, however, as the Western Christian world is concerned, the earliest clear recognition known to me that the distinction between logical and factual truth makes a certain kind of philosophical argument impossible occurs in the fourteenth century. But again it is important to make it clear that Nicolas of Autrecourt was not the only one to have argued this point effectively. Michalski has discovered many texts of other fourteenth-century writers which make the same point. There are, in fact, only two reasons to single out Autrecourt in this connection. We know that he achieved a kind of "success of scandal," and we know something of his intentions. Hence we can, in his case, distinguish what he attempted to accomplish from the intentions of positivistic thinkers in modern times from Hume to the logical positivists of the twentieth century.

The two prologues to his *Tractatus Universalis* inform us that he was attempting to show the vanity of Scholasticism. The men of his time spent many years attempting to understand and to defend some of the doctrines of Aristotle and his commentator Averroes. Autrecourt will show (1) that these doctrines are not demonstrative and (2) that an alternative metaphysics (a revision of ancient atomism) is more probable, in the light of existing knowledge, than the doctrines of Aristotle. All this is to be done for the purpose of turning men's minds and efforts to the pursuit of moral matters and to the acquisition of such little natural knowledge as men can acquire. Now there is no suggestion here of eliminating metaphysics in the interest of a rapidly developing natural science. I am not suggesting that there was no natural scientific activity in the fourteenth century. We all know better than that, in the light of the researches of Duhem and his successors. We know, too, that there was no slavish following of ancient metaphysics. But it is also true that science, in our sense,

---

1. *The Incoherence (Tahafut al-Tahafut)* of Averroes, which contains long sections of Al-Ghazali's *Tahafut al-Falasifah*, was not translated until 1328, too late to have a decisive influence. Moreover, the important last section "on the natural sciences" was not translated until much later.

involves the combination of mathematics and experimentation, which was not accomplished until the seventeenth century, however much preceding centuries had prepared the way. And we know that many of the great contributors to the seventeenth-century burst of scientific achievement felt the need for metaphysical foundations which a later positivism was to reject.

Hence, one of the main differences between the critics of metaphysics in the fourteenth century and those of modern times is that the fourteenth century had no established body of science in our sense to defend against metaphysics. Furthermore, the critics of metaphysics in the fourteenth century were, for the most part, theologians, not merely in their professional capacities but in their interests. The fourteenth-century criticism of causality and substance was contrived in the interests of Christian theology, just as Al-Ghazali's attack on the philosophers in the eleventh century had been undertaken in the interest of orthodox Islamic doctrines. The fact that views similar to or even identical with those of modern critics emerged in the process testifies to the continuity of philosophical problems, but it makes equally clear that the significance and influence of philosophical activity are largely a function of the times in which it is undertaken.

It is time, however, to turn to the substantive issues involved. As I said, the developments in logical theory by the fourteenth century made possible a relatively clear understanding of the differences between logical and factual assertions.

What can we be assured of beyond question? Autrecourt's answer is simple: as far as concerns nonpropositional cognition, of the data of outer and inner experience; as far as propositional cognition is concerned, principles known when their terms are understood, and the conclusions logically dependent upon them.[2] The vigorous adherence to this view renders certainty about causal connection or substantial existence impossible. There can be no doubt, I think, that the theological controversies of the thirteenth and fourteenth centuries were mainly responsible for this conclusion. In 1270 and 1277, the Articles of Paris condemned a number of propositions of philosophy

2. *Tractatus Universalis*, ed. J. R. O'Donnell, in "Nicholas of Autrecourt," *Mediaeval Studies*, 1 (1939), 235, ll. 6–9.

as inconsistent with Christianity. A strict adherence to Aristotle requires the denial of miracles.[3] The position of most theologians since Anselm was that God can do everything the accomplishment of which involves no contradiction. Hence any alleged demonstration that miracles are impossible must contain some flaw.[4] As Aristotle was interpreted, at least, substance must be assumed to underlie sensory experience, accidents are dependent on substance, and all events not due to chance require natural causes. Therefore Aristotle's arguments to such conclusions must contain some flaws, since if they do not, miracles are, in principle, out of the question.

Nicolas of Autrecourt argued his case as follows.[5]

The principle of contradiction lies at the foundation of valid inference. In every valid implication (*bona consequentia*) the consequent must be identical with the antecedent or, at least, with a part of what the antecedent signifies. Otherwide there would be no contradiction in asserting the antecedent and denying the consequent. Hence, from an antecedent asserting the existence of something, it is impossible to obtain a consequent asserting the existence of something else. Now it is possible, of course, to include in the meaning of one term the existence of something to which the referent of the term in question is somehow related. In this way, it might be made to appear that the existence of one thing implies that of another. But Autrecourt noticed this point in some detail. The purely verbal character of arguments which depend on defining a term so as to include in its meaning a relation to something other than the referent of the term taken precisely is elaborated in several of Autrecourt's works, in particular *The Epistles to Bernard* and *The Exigit Ordo* (or *Tractatus Universalis*). If, he argued, you restrict the terms of the antecedent of any implication to what appears in sentience, the causal characteristics of the referent of that term cannot be included

3. E.g., the Eucharist is inconsistent with Aristotle, *Physics,* Bk. I, ch. 3, 186[b] 28 ff., Bk. I, ch. 5, 188[a]-188[b]; *Daniel,* ch. 3, is incompatible with *Metaphysics* 1048[d] 5-7, Bk. IX, ch. 2, 1046[b] 18-19, and *Physics,* Bk. II, ch. 8, 199[b] 15-17.

4. Cf. Thomas Aquinas, *De Unitate Intellectus; Expositio de Trinitate,* ii, 3.

5. "Epistola Secunda ad Bernardum," ed. J. Lappe, in "Nicolaus von Autrecourt: Sein Leben, seine Philosophie, seine Schriften," *Beiträge zur Geschichte der Philosophie des Mittelalters,* vol. 6, pt. 2 (Münster, 1908), pp. 6*-14*.

in its meaning.[6] Hence, it is only by surreptitiously including in the meaning of a term more than could possibly meet the eye that an inference from one thing to another and different thing can be apparently achieved. Substance is not what appears. Neither is causal action. Therefore, neither substances nor causal connections can be guaranteed by logically certifiable inference. The empirical argument that there is nothing in the appearances which can be identified as substance or causal connection is also used.[7]

Autrecourt makes these points in detail. If whiteness is said to be an accident and an accident is defined as something existing in a subject, it follows from the existence of whiteness that a subject of inherence exists. But neither is it self-evident nor is it patent through experience that whiteness is an accident.[8] Again, if you define natural transmutation as the acquisition of something in a subject with the destruction of a prior thing in the same subject, you can formally deduce a subject of change from transmutation. But no kind of evidence is available by which we can be assured that transmutation thus conceived ever occurs. Again, if you take account only of the appearances, you may say that change can be described in the following way: a thing exists which previously did not exist. From such a description, a substratum cannot be inferred.[9]

6. This point was anticipated by Ockham. *Ordinatio in Librum Primum Sententiarum*, Prol., q. 9: "However often one experiences in himself that he knows something perfectly and intuitively, he never knows something else by means of this knowledge unless he previously has also had knowledge of that other thing." (For Latin text see *Guillelmi de Ockham Opera Philosophica et Theologica. Opera Theologica*, vol. I [St. Bonaventure, N.Y.: Franciscan Institute, 1967], p. 241.) In his *Expositio super Octo Libros Physicorum* (Berlin, Staatsbibl. Ms. Elect. 974, fol. 113^r) and in *Ordinatio*, dist. 3, q. 2 (*Opera Theologica*, II, 414) Ockham defines knowing a thing perfectly as "notice of its intrinsic causes, namely of matter and form and knowledge of integral parts suffices for perfect knowledge of a thing, because in this knowledge it suffices to know all that which is of the nature and essence of the thing." References from L. Baudry, *Lexique philosophique de Guillaume d'Ockham* (Paris, 1958), pp. 178-79. Moreover, for Ockham, knowledge of causal efficacy requires experience. See *Summa Logicae*, III, pt. 2, ch. 10; *Ordinatio*, Prol., q. 2 (*Opera Theologica*, I, 90-95); *Expositio super Octo Libros Physicorum*, fol. 122^V.

7. "Epistola Nicholai ad Egidium," ed. J. Lappe, in "Nicolaus von Autrecourt," p. 28*, ll. 25–26, and p. 29*, ll. 1–20.

8. Ibid., p. 28*, ll. 25-26.

9. *Tractatus Universalis*, ed. O'Donnell, p. 192, l. 10, p. 193, l. 9.

Now it will perhaps be suggested that the Christian Aristotelians knew all this. St. Thomas, for example, was certainly aware of the fact that the miraculous intervention of God made it imperative to qualify the maxims of Aristotle about natural necessity and about the relation of substance and accident, and the like.[10] He also knew that we rarely can claim a knowledge of the essence of things in nature and so have to take accidents in place of the less-accessible substantial forms.[11] At the same time, St. Thomas also held that we can 'and do arrive at the knowledge of essences of things, even though inference (discourse) is required for this.[12] It is also true that Duns Scotus, who was generally more careful than the theologians who wrote before 1277, supposed that it is possible to achieve certainty by means of natural knowledge (i.e., without special illumination). But the analytic character of the propositions by which this is achieved was fully exposed by the critics in the fourteenth century. Besides, Scotus' arguments involving causality require a preamble derived from observation,[13] and the question whether "being effected" is applicable to anything presented in experience, is not answered. It was this question which was pressed by some of the fourteenth-century critics of natural knowledge. If anyone doubts that this was the case, the texts published by Michalski should be convincing.

Another feature of philosophy in the fourteenth century, perhaps one which had the greatest influence on subsequent thought, is the development of nominalism. This is difficult to characterize in general because the nominalists differed among themselves on important issues, particularly on the notion of *relation*. Thus whereas a particular view of relations lies at the basis of Ockham's nominalism, it does

10. *De Potentia Dei; Summa Theologiae,* Part I, q. 25; *Summa contra Gentiles,* iii, 99-102.

11. *Summa Theologiae,* Part I, q. 77, a. 1, ad 7[m], and Part I, q. 18, a. 2; *In Posterior Analytics,* lect. 13; *Summa contra Gentiles,* i, 3, and iv, 1; *Expositio in Symb. Apost.,* q. 2.

12. *Scriptum in Libros Sententiarum,* iii, d. 35, q. 2, a. 2, sol. 1; *De Ente et Essentia,* ch. 6.

13. *De primo Principio,* ed. Evan Roche, Franciscan Institute Publications, Philosophy Series, no. 5 (St. Bonaventure, N.Y., 1949), p. 40. Cf. Petrus Thomas, as quoted by Ignatius Brady, *Proceedings of the American Catholic Philosophical Association,* 28 (1954), 124-25.

not seem to be central to the views of either Aureoli or Durandus on the problem of universals. So I shall not attempt to speak of fourteenth-century nominalism in general but only in the form given by Ockham.

There are many features of Ockham's nominalism which, superficially, seem doctrinally allied to views which have been championed by positivists of the twentieth century and by their eighteenth- and nineteenth-century predecessors. This is, in part, an illusion. Ockham's nominalism, as Vignaux has copiously shown,[14] was undertaken in the interest of his own version of the substance-accident ontology. It was certainly not prompted by a general attack on metaphysics, but on the contrary was pursued in the interests of metaphysics which Ockham thought to be authentically Aristotelian. The development of the doctrines of signification and supposition, the ruthless application of the principle of thought economy and of the theological principle that God can do whatever does not involve contradiction, all these enter into Ockham's complex theory of universals as concepts rather than extraconceptual realities. Yet it is correct to describe Ockham's fundamental views on universals and intuitive knowledge as "realistic" in the sense defined by the late Philotheus Boehner.[15] Ockham's nominalism or conceptualism had as its principal aim the emphatic affirmation of the reality of individuals (substances and qualities), and his emphasis on intuitive knowledge was intended to establish our direct knowledge of extramental reality. It is this, in fact, on which his rejection of intelligible species depends.

It is true, of course, that a simpler metaphysics emerges from the rejection of Scotus' common natures. It is true, too, that the rejection of many other features of Scotus' philosophy on the basis of economy seem something like later discussions. Some writers have seen in their "reduction of entities" anticipations of Russell's doctrine to replace inferred entities by logical constructions. But

14. "Nominalisme," *Dictionnaire de theologie catholique*, 11/1 (Paris, 1930), cols. 717–84; *Nominalisme au XIVᵉ siècle* (Montreal, 1948).

15. "The Realistic Conceptualism of William Ockham," *Traditio*, 4 (1946), 307-35; first part reprinted in *Collected Articles on Ockham*, Franciscan Institute Publications, Philosophy Series, no. 12 (St. Bonaventure, N.Y., 1958), pp. 156-74.

whereas Russell argues that this can be managed only by the logic of relations and by the admission that relations are a part of the ultimate furniture of the world, Ockham thought that it could be done only by rejecting the extramental status of relations. The difference, however, does not end here. Ockham and the other medieval followers of Aristotle had nothing of the modern conception of relations, but his principles would have obliged him to reject the modern view had it ever been suggested to him.

Ockham (and his followers in the fourteenth century) discovered a way to reduce the number of things assumed in physical theory. Some terms of discourse have only a nominal essence. Such terms as motion, place, and time can be so treated. They are really only abbreviations for prolix formulae. To say that there is motion is an abbreviation for the more prolix statement that a movable thing successively occupies different places at different times. This has reminded many of Russell's attempt to replace inferred entities by logical constructions. But there are important differences. It is true that both philosophers invoke the principle of parsimony. Yet one of them, Ockham, was engaged in the wholesale reduction of entities in the interest of the doctrine of substance, whereas Russell was attempting to destroy the traditional concept of substance. Moreover, Ockham supposes that his reduction of entities depends, in part at least, on a denial of the extracognitive reality of relations, whereas Russell's chief insistence was that relations as extracognitive features of reality are the essential constituents of his logical constructions. If the ultimate result of Ockham's work was the denial of substance, it was as far from Ockham's intentions as can be imagined.

The truth of the matter seems to me to be this: the program of Ockham could only have been carried out by means of a view of relations which Ockham formally and explicitly rejected. As this matter is of great theoretical importance, I propose to go into it more thoroughly here.

I have asserted elsewhere[16] that the medievals had no satisfactory theory of relations. Mr. Geach, in a review, has countered with a number of citations from medieval authors. I believe, however, that close inspection of medieval discussions of relations will reveal that I was not mistaken. The Aristotelian categories include the category

16. *Nicolaus of Autrecourt* (Princeton, 1948).

of πρός τι, it is true, But relations are accidents, and an accident cannot belong to two subjects. Hence, either relations are purely *entia rationis*, or, if they have a foundation *in re*, they are special kinds of inhering accidents. Ockham's whole attack against Scotus' view depends on treating relations as inhering accidents and then arguing that, since accidents are absolutes and hence separable from their substrata *per potentiam Dei absolutam*, relational accidents could so exist. Because this is manifestly absurd, Ockham concludes against relational accidents and hence against the extramental or extradiscursive reality of relations. Others who held the view that relations are inhering accidents (but who rejected some of the other assumptions made by Ockham) concluded that some relations are extramental and that they are inhering accidents of a special kind. There, I think, are the facts of the case.

If I am correct, the Ockhamite program of reducing the number of entities was motivated by an attempt to save the phenomena with substance and quality alone. If we see that a satisfactory account of motion can be effected only by assuming the extramental existence of relations conceived as connections of two or more terms, then Ockham's program must be pronounced a failure. To this extent, the "positivism" of the fourteenth century must be conceived as fundamentally different from that of the twentieth.

The critique of Scholastic method, as has often been indicated, had one of its roots in the theological controversies culminating in the condemnation of 1277 (the so-called Articles of Paris). Yet the articulate form of that critique owed much to the increasing understanding of formal logic which was accomplished by the fourteenth-century logicians. Building on the foundation of Aristotle's *Organon* and, very indirectly, on the work of the Megarian-Stoic logician of the fourth century B.C., the logicians of the fourteenth century investigated syllogistic reasoning, the logic of modalities, but also and more important, the logic of consequence. Doubtless, the work of earlier medieval logicians had paved the way for this. Anselm's "necessary reasons,"[17] Abelard's discussions in "Logica Ingredientibus" of the necessity of consequence,[18] Peter of Spain's doctrine

17. *Monologium*, Praef.; chs. 2, 7, 64.

18. *"Glossa in* ΠΕΡΙ ΕΡΜΗ," ed. B. Geyer, in *Beiträge zur Geschichte der Philosophie des Mittelalters*, vol. 6, pt. 3 (Münster, 1927), pp. 366, 367, 496, and passim.

of the natural, contingent, or remote "matter" of propositions (which is derived from the twelfth-century logicians)[19] all anticipate the precise formulations of the nature of *consequence* (*implication* in modern terminology) in the fourteenth century. Al-Ghazali had already defended the radical view that necessity and impossibility amount to nothing more than the denial and affirmation of contradiction.[20] Moreover, some of the thirteenth-century writers had made it plain that in some way, all principles are reducible to the principle of noncontradiction, and that absolute necessity and impossibility are indefinable in terms of contradiction.[21]

Nevertheless, the definitions of necessity and impossibility in the fourteenth century show, I think, a great precision and awareness of the issues which are settled by such definitions. Thus Ockham's "absolute necessity is when something is unqualifiedly necessary such that the supposition that its opposite is true contains a contradiction."[22] The definitions of formal, material, and "as of now" consequences all depend on this conception of necessity. One of the earlier statements of the nature of consequence is in pseudo-Scotus (John of Cornwall) to the following effect:[23] "It is necessary and sufficient for the validity of a consequence that it is impossible . . . for the antecedent to be true and the consequent false . . . when a consequent follows from an antecedent the opposite of the consequent is inconsistent with the antecedent." Another is Raymond Lull:[24] "For the truth of a conditional, it is required that the antecedent cannot hold without the consequent, e.g., Thou art a man, therefore a being. To know this it must be observed whether the opposite of the consequent is inconsistent with [*repugnat*] the antecedent. Now for the falsity [of a conditional] it is required that the

19. *Summulae Logicales*, 1, 2, 3; John of Salisbury, *Metalogicon*, i, 15.

20. In Averroes, *Tahafut al-Tahafut*, trans S. van den Bergh (London, 1954), I, 329.

21. Thomas Aquinas, *Summa Theologiae*, Part I, q. 25, a. 31, and Part I, q. 19, a. 3; *Summa contra Gentiles*, ii, 25; John Duns Scotus, *Opus Oxoniense*, I, d. 3, q. 4, a. 2.

22. *Quodlibeta Septem*, vi, q. 2; cf. Gabriel Biel, *Collectorium*, dist. 17, q. 1.

23. *Quaestiones in Librum Primorum Analyticorum Aristotelis*, q. 10 in *Opera Omnia I. D. Scoti* (Lyon, 1639), I, 286-89; (Paris, 1891), II, 103-8.

24. *Logica*, ch. 7: "De Propositione," in *Opera ea Quae ad Inventam ab ipso Artem Universalem Pertinent* (Strasbourg, 1598), p. 159.

antecedent can hold without the consequent, even that it can be seen by observing that the opposite of the consequent is not inconsistent with [*non repugnat*] the antecedent."

Ralph Strode, in his "Consequentiae et Obligationes,"[25] has a similar description of the truth of conditionals and consequences, and Walter Burleigh, "De Puritate Artis Logicae Tractatus Longior,"[26] states, "Whatever stands with the antecedent stands with the consequent, and I mean by the phrase 'to stand with something' to be able to be true with it. Whence for some things to stand together is the same as that it is not inconsistent for them to be true together," and "in every valid consequence, the opposite of the consequent is inconsistent with the antecedent . . . all inconsistency holds in virtue of contradiction."[27]

Some historians of medieval logic[28] have argued that the fourteenth-century logicians had arrived at the conception of a material conditional. But none of the examples which they cite are material conditionals in our sense. All of them are cases in which the conditional is logically true because the consequent is necessary or because the antecedent is impossible. If we consult other authors, Albert of Saxony or Walter Burleigh, for example, the matter seems beyond question. Albert of Saxony[29] says explicitly that "every true conditional is necessary and every false conditional is impossible." As a matter of fact, Philo of Megara seems to have been the only author who can possibly be said to have known what a material conditional was (in the modern sense, of course). The medievals speak of a "material consequence," but this is another thing. In any case, it was the precise definition of consequence which enabled many fourteenth-century theologians and philosophers to show

25. *Consequentiae Strodi cum Commento Alexandri Sermoneta* (Venice, 1493), fol. 28.

26. *De Puritate Artis Logicae Tractatus Longior,* Franciscan Institute Publications, Text Series, no. 9 (St. Bonaventure, N.Y., 1955), p. 63.

27. *Expositio. . . in Libros Octo de Physico* (Venice, 1482), fol. 138^V.

28. For example, E. A. Moody, *The Logic of William of Ockham* (London, 1935), p. 287; Philotheus Boehner, "Does Ockham Know of Material Implication," *Franciscan Studies,* 11 (1951), 203-30; reprinted in *Collected Articles on Ockham,* pp. 319-51.

29. *Summa Logicae,* Tr. IV, ch. 1.

more conclusively that a logical connection among distinct things was impossible.

But there were other aspects of logical theory in the fourteenth century which were important in this connection. The verbal character of certain arguments which were characteristic of Scholastic metaphysics was revealed by the increasing use of the distinction between nominal and real definitions, or, as the Scholastics put it, between the *quid nominis* and the *quid rei*. This is perhaps best illustrated by Ockham's elucidation of motion, place, time, etc. According to the Venerable Inceptor, *motion* has only a *quid nominis*, a nominal meaning, and is an abbreviation for a prolix formula stating that a body is successively in several positions or (in the case of mutation) is successively in different conditions. This was maintained in the interests of Ockham's nominalistic metaphysics and was supported, *inter alia*, by the maxim of thought economy as well as by the theological principle of divine omnipotence. The adoption of Ockham's theory of motion by some of the younger Parisian masters such as Nicolas of Autrecourt had other motivations, and its probable influence on the study of the kinematical aspects of motion by some of the members of Merton College should not obscure the fact that Ockham did not intend any positivistic approach to scientific questions.

Still another consequence of the intensive cultivation of logical studies in the fourteenth century was the increasing use of probable arguments.[30] The notion of the "probable" as frequency of events as well as argument based on widely held opinions comes from Aristotle, but it was the latter sense of "probable" which occurs most often in the writings of the fourteenth century. Consequent on the ever more widely held view that there are few or no conclusive arguments in metaphysical matters was the view that metaphysical and physical questions admit only of a probable resolution. We find this tendency illustrated in Ockham, and more fully in Autrecourt, Mirecourt, and many other writers whose works have been examined as yet incompletely. It is particularly strong in Pierre d'Ailly, who comes at the end of the century, and the use of the method of probable

30. See L. Baudry, *Lexique philosophique de Guillaume d'Ockham*, pp. 216–17.

argument is well known in Nicolas or Oreseme's commentary on *De Caelo*.

The realization that even probable arguments are hardly available for certain purposes is illustrated by several authors. Nicolas of Autrecourt, for example, says that, in the sense in which probability depends on the observation of previous conjunctions in our experience, there are not even probable arguments for substances.[31] As there is no observed conjunction *in experience* between substance and its alleged appearances, there can be no probability of the existence of substance given any appearances. This argument is precisely the argument of Hume[32] to the same effect. Those who reject this extreme view nevertheless raise questions about the allegedly direct knowledge of matter. Thus the author of the commentary on the *Physics* (included in the Wadding edition of Scotus but early ascribed to Marsilius of Inghen)[33] argues that prime matter is only known by inference and that although such inferences are not demonstrative, they are more probable than other ways of "saving" generation and corruption. Again Walter Burleigh[34] argues that our knowledge of nature (in the Aristotelian sense of nature as a source of being moved, etc.) is not self-evident but rather obtained by an "imperceptible" inference. More radical views were expressed by Mirecourt, Richard Fitz-Ralph, and others. In a number of cases, like that of Mirecourt, there is a three-fold distinction of evidence, viz., absolutely conclusive evidence, natural evidence, and probability. But the overall impression one obtains from reading the fourteenth-century Scholastics is the increasing realization that absolute evidence is limited to the immediate data of consciousness, the self-evidence of propositions depending only on the meaning of their terms and the conclusions which follow deductively therefrom.[35]

31. *Epistola secunda ad Bernardum,* ed. J. Lappe, *Nicolaus von Autrecourt,* p. 13*, ll. 3-19.

32. *Enquiry Concerning Human Understanding,* sec. 12, pt. 1, par. 12.

33. *Opera Omnia I. D. Scoti,* II, 84.

34. *Expositio . . . in Libros Physicorum* (Venice, 1482), pp. 145–46.

35. Nicolaus of Autrecourt, *Tractatus universalis,* ed. O'Donnell, p. 235, ll. 6-9. John of Mirecourt, "In Libros Sententiarum," L. I, q. 6, in *Questioni inedite di Giovanni de Mirecourt sulla cognascenza,* ed. A. Franzinelli, Rivista critica di storia della filosofia, Anno XIII (Florence, 1958), pp. 437-49.

The "probabilism" of the fourteenth century must, I am still convinced, be distinguished from the doctrine attributed to some thirteenth-century masters by the Articles of Paris and sometimes called the doctrine of double truth. It may well be the case that recent researches have failed to turn up anyone who maintained explicitly that the theological truth and philosophical truth are incompatible. But certainly there is a plain difference between holding that some demonstrable statements in natural philosophy are inconsistent with faith and holding that some probable statements are inconsistent with faith. The human targets of the Articles of Paris seem to have held to the former of these views, whereas the decrees of 1339 and 1340 of the University of Paris, and the condemnations of Autrecourt and Morecourt, were directed against the latter view.

What was the doctrine which we can call probabilism? It seems to consist of two parts. First, the contention that intuition and demonstration cannot establish the principles of metaphysics or the principles and conclusions of natural science. Second, that metaphysics and natural science consists mainly or wholly of "probable arguments," "persuasions," and "sufficient proofs." These are, in principle, the probabilities, the *Endoxa* of Aristotle. But whereas Aristotle, at least as he was interpreted in the thirteenth and fourteenth centuries, held that some of the assumptions of first philosophy and physics are beyond question, the probabilists of the fourteenth century held that such principles belong to the realm of opinion rather than to sapience or science. This view of the matter is historically confirmed, so it appears to me, by the explicit statements of Autrecourt, Mirecourt, d'Ailly, and especially Pierre de Ceffons,[36] who makes it perfectly clear that probability is not the same as truth, so that some false propositions are more probable than their true contradictories.

It was in terms of probable arguments that Autrecourt defended atomism and that Oresme defended a theory of the movement of the earth. It should be noted, though, that traditional positions were also defended on probable grounds in lieu of intuition or demonstration.

36. K. Michalski, *Le problème de la volonté à Oxford et à Paris au XIVe siècle*, Studia Philosophica: Commentarii Societatis Philosophicae Polonorum, II (Lemberg, 1937), 360.

Still another feature of some fourteenth-century discussions may be noticed. Autrecourt calls attention to the fact that in an account of the nature of things which claims to be only probable at best, it is legitimate to make use of what he called "external similitudes."[37] "For those things which do not fall under the scrutiny of the senses are not conceived by proper essential concepts. Wherefore an explication can only be made according to some external similitudes." This applies no less to the relation of acts of cognition to the cognizing soul than to the relation of inherence between the accidents and their substantial supports. Since we abstract the concept of inherence from such observable connections as that of skin to flesh and bones and afterwards apply this abstraction to the connection of accidents to substances, we do not really know whether or to what extent the concept applies. We are dealing with an analogy which is obviously external, since the connection of accident and substance is never the direct object of inspection. This critique of metaphysical concepts does not seem to be intended as an outright rejection of such concepts as being wholly without meaning. It is a warning, rather than an indictment or a conviction. In fact, there is no suggestion of a phenomenalistic rejection of metaphysics, but rather only a further argument to support the contention that metaphysical statements can, at best, be only probable.

Let me consider the problem of causal connection as it was treated by many of the fourteenth-century authors. Ockham certainly doubted that an absolute proof can be given that there are any second causes.[38] This view is reiterated, sometimes in a more radical form, by Autrecourt, Mirecourt, Holcot, and many others. The question here is, of course, whether a demonstration of causal connection can be given. Yet neither Ockham nor his more radical successors doubted that there is causal connection.[39] Ockham, for instance, makes the matter rest on "experience," and in particular, on the method of difference.[40] Autrecourt argues that causal efficacy can be determined with probability from the operations of natural

37. *Tractatus Universalis,* p. 225, l. 38.
38. *In Librum Secundum Sententiarum,* q. 5, R.
39. See L. Baudry, *Lexique philosophique,* pp. 40-41; Ockham, *In Librum Secundum Sententiarum*, qq. 14-15.
40. *In Librum Primum Sententiarum,* dist. 45, q. unica et passim.

things. Here again, there is no suggestion that there is no causal connection, but only that our cognition of it is probable and wholly dependent on experience. While there can be no doubt that the tone of caution in the fourteenth century is noticeably great, and different from the sometimes jaunty assurance encountered in the thirteenth century, there is no suggestion that causal connection is merely the uniform and invariable sequence of eighteenth- and nineteenth-century empiricism or twentieth-century positivism.

Some final remarks on this subject should be added. Autrecourt criticizes Scotus' argument that certitude is obtainable by the method of agreement and the principle that what occurs, as in many cases, from a non-free cause is its natural effect. He points out the verbal character of Scotus' use of this causal maxim, and then asserts that things known by experience are known only by a "conjecturative habit" rather than by any certitude. At first sight this sounds like Hume. But whereas Hume concludes that the felt force of habituation explains the illusion of a necessary connection in the events themselves, Autrecourt does not further develop the idea that causal beliefs are only habits productive of conjecture. And it is clear why this is so. Autrecourt is not concerned to reject the metaphysical notion of cause but is concerned only to point out the limits of our knowledge with regard to that relation.

The foregoing observations tend to show, I think, that the motives and the achievements of fourteenth-century critics of metaphysical knowledge were quite different from the motives and results of the positivists of the twentieth century. Certainly there are important resemblances. The understanding of logical necessity and the consequent limits of reason and experience are, broadly speaking, similar in the fourteenth and twentieth centuries. The substitution of logical constructions for inferred entities recommended by Russell and later taken up by members of the Vienna circle has a sort of counterpart in Ockham's treatment of motion. But the differences begin to appear. For the suggestion that metaphysics is nonsense does not seem to have been made by those fourteenth-century philosophers, whereas it certainly was the battlecry of the logical positivists.

I do not want to be misunderstood. The particular results obtained by the study of a philosophical problem in widely separated periods by men with radically different intentions may yet be sufficiently similar for us to derive similar illumination from them. But what we can learn from the study of the history of thought and what that history itself contains are inevitably different. The attempt to assimilate the thought of the past to that of the present by a rational *Umdeutung* can only be prompted by the egotism of our own time and can only lead to confusion.

II
MODERN
PHILOSOPHY

6
Descartes on the Distinction of Mind and Body

It can be shown that Descartes has two different arguments for the distinction of mind and body: (1) It is possible, i.e. involves no contradiction, to think that I, as thinking, exist and that nothing extended exists, and since the existence, power, and veracity of God assures me that God can bring about whatever I can conceive, it is therefore possible that I exist without a body. Hence, body and mind are really distinct. (2) The essence or attribute of nature which is thought (*cogitatio*) is logically incompatible with that of extension. Hence these attributes cannot belong to one substance but only to two. There has been some debate about whether these arguments are really distinct, but it is clear, historically speaking, that the second argument is independent of the first, because it was proposed by a number of philosophers long before the seventeenth century and urged on a variety of grounds. It is presented by Descartes in the sixth meditation as a distinct argument: "quod unum sufficeret ad me docendum, mentem a corpore omnino esse diversam, si nondum illud aliunde satis scirem," a statement which also clearly implies that the first argument is independent of the second.[1] It is, however,

1. *Oeuvres de Descartes*, ed. C. Adam and P. Tannery (Paris: Cerf, 1897-1913), VII, 86[13-15]. (Cited hereafter as *AT*, with volume number.) Reprinted by Vrik, 1957-58. Cf. *The Philosophical Works of Descartes*, trans. E. S. Haldane and G. R. T. Ross, 2 vols. (1911; Cambridge: Cambridge University Press, 1967), I, 196. (Cited hereafter as *HR*.)

worth remarking that in his correspondence, Descartes sometimes runs the two together.

Descartes' interest in the proof of a real distinction between mind and body is, at least, twofold. On the one hand, it forms the basis of a proof of the immortality of the soul which, however, Descartes later thought was impossible to bring off.[2] At best, we can prove the possibility of immortality, but natural reason cannot assure us that Omnipotence will or must accomplish what Omnipotence can accomplish, so that the final assurance of the permanent survival of the soul must come from revelation.

On the other hand, Cartesian dualism opens the way to a purely physical or even mechanical account of the physiology of the human body and, indeed, a purely physical account of the natural world. That this account of the physical world led eventually to a form of materialism in eighteenth-century French philosophy is well known, but as far from Descartes' intention as can be imagined.

In order to understand these arguments, it is advisable to investigate their historical background. Descartes sometimes wrote as if he were a complete innovator in this matter. "For no one before me, so far as I know, asserted that mind consisted in one thing alone, namely the faculty of thinking and the inward source [of thinking]."[3] Sometimes he expressly dissociates his usages from those of the Schoolmen, although at other times he expressly employs their terminology. But it has been copiously shown by Gilson and others that his thought and expression are deeply rooted in medieval thought, and we must delve into some of the ideas of the Scholastics in order to ascertain exactly what Descartes meant by many or most of the things he said.

Let me begin with the first argument, that mind and body are really distinct because I can conceive of the one apart from the other. We must be careful to distinguish two senses in which this might be meant: (1) I can think of the quality or attribute of thought without thinking of anything else, and in particular without thinking of any material thing or of the attribute of extension; (2) When I think of both thought and extension I can perceive clearly and distinctly

2. II^{ae} Resp., *HR*, II, 47.

3. *Notae in Programma*; *HR*, I, 434; *AT*, VII^{ae} Resp. *HR*, II, 335; *AT*, VII, 549$^{20-21}$.

that they can exist apart, either one separated from the other or one existing and the other not existing. It is amply clear that the first interpretation must be rejected on Descartes' own showing. He was aware that nothing of importance follows from the fact that I can think of *a* without thinking of *b*. For by an abstraction which, in fact, renders a concept inadequate, I can think of *a* without thinking of *b* even if *a* and *b* are necessarily connected. Descartes, then, evidently has meaning 2 in mind.

The hyperbolic doubt enables me to conceive of the possibility that I, as thinking, exist and that no material thing exists. If there were a contradiction in holding that I am thinking and not extended, there would also be a contradiction in holding that I think and no extended thing exists. For if *a* yields *b* and *b* is a contradiction, so is *a*, and so if *a* yields *b* and *a* is not a contradiction, then *b* is not a contradiction.

Why, however, is Descartes so sure that the hyperbolic doubt is free from contradiction? It is because he is sure of the following three propositions: (1) I clearly and distinctly conceive myself as thinking; (2) I have a clear and distinct conception of extension, that is, of an extended thing or a complete being, which means of an extended thing as capable of existing without anything else (excepting the concourse of God); (3) I can entertain the idea of myself existing and no extended thing existing. But is this enough? Is it not possible that there is something about me that escapes detection? May not this, after all, be a material thing? The fact that I can conceive of matter existing without thinking does not imply that thinking can exist without matter. Perhaps, after all, the hyperbolic doubt is really impossible. In order to dispel these doubts, it is necessary to examine Descartes' several statements and to investigate what meanings he associated with these statements. In Part IV of the *Discourse*, Descartes holds that "from [the fact that I can conceive I have no body etc.] I knew that I was a substance the whole essence of which is to think, and that for its existence there is no need of any place, nor does it depend on any material thing, so that this 'me', that is to say the soul . . . is entirely distinct from body. . . ."[4]

In the *Search after Truth* (the date of which is uncertain), ". . . I exist and am not a body; otherwise, doubting of my body I should

4. *HR*, I, 101.

at the same time doubt of myself."[5] It is clear that these statements as they stand do not dispel the aforementioned doubts, already suggested by critics of the *Discourse*. Descartes alludes to this in the *Preface to the Reader of the Meditations*. Here he is more cautious and makes it clear that the Divine Guarantee is required to complete the proof of the real distinction. Here it is only in the order of his thought that "so far as I was aware, I knew nothing clearly as belonging to my essence, excepting that I was a thing which thinks, or a thing that has in itself the faculty of thinking. But I shall show hereafter how from the fact that I know no other thing which pertains to my essence, it follows that there is no other thing that really does belong to it."[6]

These remarks mean that the real distinction of mind and body, suggested in the second meditation, is not completed until the sixth meditation with the Divine Guarantee already at hand. The Divine Veracity guarantees that whatever things I can conceive as existing apart from one another (either in the sense of mutual separation or in the sense that either exists without the existence of the other), are within the power of God to make to exist apart whether God does this by an ordinary or an extraordinary exercise of His power. The full force of this use of the Divine Veracity is brought out most clearly in a letter to P. Gibieuf: "Of all those things of which we have diverse and complete ideas . . . it implies a contradiction that they are inseparable. Yet I do not deny that there can be in the soul or in the body many properties of which I have no idea; I deny only that there are any which are inconsistent with those I have of them, and, among the others, inconsistent with the idea I have of their distinction. Otherwise God would be a deceiver, and we would have no rule to assure us of the truth."[7] The Divine Veracity guarantees the truth of evidence. If it is evident to me that body and mind are complete things so that no contradiction is apparent if I suppose they can exist apart, indeed, if there is a contradiction in supposing

5. Ibid., 319.
6. Ibid., 138; cf. *AT*, VII, 226[8-26]; *HR*, II, 97-102; *AT*, VII, 357-20; *HR*, II, 230-31.
7. Descartes to P. Gibieuf, 19 January 1642, *Descartes Oeuvres et Lettres* (Editions Gallimard, 1953), p. 1142.

that the separable is inseparable, only then can I be sure that mind and body are really distinct.[8]

Descartes' fullest and most systematic account of this argument is to be found in the *Geometrical Exposition* appended to the *Replies to the Second Objections*.[9] Two substances are called really distinct when each of them can exist apart from the other. The ultimate source of this phrase "real distinction" is Aristotle: "moreover, if one thing can exist without the other, the former will not be the same as the latter."[10] It came to Descartes, most probably, by way of Suarez and some of the other sixteenth-century Scholastics. According to Suarez, the real distinction "consists in the fact that one thing is not another."[11] A sign of the real distinction is the fact that "two objective concepts are capable of separation in nature and in the concrete individual such that either one (of the two) can exist and the other not exist or one is really disjoined from the other."[12] To this Suarez adds that there is no point to asking whether such separation takes place naturally or in virtue of the absolute power of God.[13] But, where two things are naturally conjoined, there is no unusual sign of such a real distinction and "we must examine each instance in the light of the essential nature proper to it, its degree of perfection, and the function to which it is ordained, so that from all these together we may form a judgment on the distinction."[14] It is clear that Descartes could have made little use of this last remark as it stands, but the injunction to examine the essential nature would not have escaped his notice. So much, then, for the meaning of a *real* distinction.

The second point made in the *Geometrical Exposition* is that whatever we clearly perceive can be made by God just as we perceive it. This is proved by the Corollary to Proposition 3, which is to the

---

8. Meditation vi, *HR*, I, 190.
9. *Geometrical Exposition*, Def. x.
10. *Topics*, vii, 1, 152^b, 34-35.
11. *Disputationes Metaphysicae*, VII, sec. 1, par. 1.
12. Ibid., sec. 2, par. 2.
13. Ibid., par. 10.
14. Ibid., par. 21.

effect that in proving the existence of God, I have proved the existence of all those things which I conceive to be possible.[15]

Now we clearly see that the mind is such that it can exist apart from or without a body, for Postulate 2 of the *Geometrical Exposition* asks us to study the mind and the attributes so that we can see that it can be known, assuming that no bodies exist. Conversely, it is generally admitted that bodies can exist without mind. It follows that at least by virtue of divine power or omnipotence mind can exist without body and conversely. Substances that can exist, one apart from the other, either in actual separation or in that one can exist and the other fail to exist, are really distinct. Mind and body being substances, they can exist apart from each other. This is precisely the conclusion of Meditation vi, that "because I know that all things which I apprehend clearly and distinctly can be created by God as I apprehend them, it suffices that I am able to apprehend one thing apart from another in order to be certain that the one is different from the other, since they can be made to exist in separation at least by the omnipotence of God."[16]

The *Principles*, generally speaking, confirm all this and especially reiterate the point that the best way to distinguish mind from body is by way of the discovery of our own existence when we doubt that any extended things exist. For while we still doubt that there are other things in the world, we know that we think.[17] We are further informed that our thought must belong to something,[18] which turns out to be a substance in the sense defined by *Principles*, I, 51. Each substance, moreover, has a principal attribute on which all its other properties depend. Now the principal attribute of mind is thought,[19] for as we can conceive of thinking without imagination or sensation (but not conversely), it is clear that the latter depend on the former, that is, are modes of the former,[20] and so differ from thought[21] by a

15. *AT*, VII, 169$^{14-18}$, *HR*, II, 58, 59.
16. *HR*, I, 190; cf. *HR*, II, 54.
17. *Principles of Philosophy*, Part I, Principle 8; *HR*, I, 221.
18. *Principles*, I, 11; *HR*, I, 223.
19. *Principles*, 53; *HR*, I, 240.
20. *Principles*, I, 56; *HR*, I, 241, 242.
21. *Principles*, I, 59, 60; *HR*, I, 242-44.

modal distinction merely. Here Descartes' doctrine is again derived from Suarez[22] as a simple comparison of texts shows.

In the *Principles* and *Replies to Objections*, Descartes explains with some detail the difference between abstraction and distinction or exclusion. As he puts it in a letter to P. Mesland (2 May 1644, Pleiade 1168): "There is a great difference between *abstraction* and *exclusion*. If I were just saying that my idea of my soul does not represent it as dependent on the body or identical with the body, that would be *abstraction*, from which I could frame only an inconclusive argument. What I do say is that the idea represents the soul as a substance that may exist even after the exclusion of whatever belongs to the body; from this I frame a positive argument, and conclude that soul can exist without body. The way extension is excluded by the nature of the soul is seen clearly in the impossibility of conceiving half a conscious being [chose qui pense] as you rightly remark."

Abstraction allows us to conceive one thing without conceiving another, an operation which not only does not guarantee that the one conceived can exist without the other which was not conceived, but was usually thought of by the medievals as an operation by which the mind can think apart what cannot, indeed, exist apart. That this was the meaning of *abstraction* I have made out at length elsewhere.[23] Now, Descartes frequently insists that abstraction renders our concepts inadequate and so reduces or eliminates their distinctness, which is a condition for Descartes of *evident* knowledge. Although none of our concepts is entirely adequate in the sense that we know everything about mind or body, nevertheless we can have a concept sufficiently adequate when we can see whether we are not or are conceiving of something as a complete or as an incomplete reality.

As he wrote to P. Gibieuf,

> As for the principle by which it seems that I know that the idea I have of a thing is not made inadequate by an abstraction

22. *Disputationes Metaphysicae*, VII, sec. 2, par. 6.
23. *Abstraction, Relation, and Induction* (Madison: University of Wisconsin Press, 1965).

of the mind I derived it only from my own thought or consciousness. For being assured that I have knowledge of that which is external to me, only by the mediation of ideas which I have had in myself, I am careful not to relate my judgments immediately to things and attribute nothing positive to them which I do not previously perceive in their ideas; but I believe too, that whatever is found in these ideas is necessarily in things. And so, in order to know whether my idea is not rendered incomplete or *inadequate* [Latin] by some abstraction of the mind, I take care merely to see that I have not taken it (not from something external to me which may be more complete) but from some other idea more ample or more complete which is *in* me by an abstraction of the mind, i.e., by turning my thought away from that part of what is contained in this more ample idea in order to apply it somewhat better and to make me more attentive to the other part. Thus when I consider a figure without thinking of the substance or extension of which it is a figure, I make an abstraction of the mind which I can easily recognize later, by asking whether I have not taken this idea which I have of a figure alone from some other more ample idea which I also have in myself, with which it is so connected that, even though I can think of the one without giving any attention to the other, I cannot in any case deny that it belongs to the other when I think of the two together. For I see clearly that the idea of the figure is so connected to the idea of extension and of a substance, in view of the fact that it is impossible that I conceive a figure while denying that it has an extension, or that I conceive of an extension while denying that it is the extension of a substance.

However, the idea of an extended and figured substance is complete, because I can conceive it altogether alone and deny of it all other things of which I have the idea. Now it is, so it seems to me, quite clear that the idea which I have of a substance which thinks is complete in this way; and that I have no other idea which precedes it in my mind and to which it is so conjoined that I cannot easily think of them while denying one of the other. For if there were any such in me, I should know it. Someone will perhaps say that the difficulty still remains because, even though I conceive soul and body as two substances so that I conceive one without the other, and even to the point of denying one of the other, I am still not assured that they are such as I conceive them. But it is necessary in this matter to hark back to the rule previously set forth, namely, that we are not able to have any knowledge of things save by way of the ideas that we condeive of them; and, hence, that we should only judge of them according to these ideas, and indeed, we should think that whatever is inconsistent with these ideas is absolutely impossible and implies contradiction.

Thus we have no reason to be assured that there is no mountain without a valley, save that we see that their ideas could not be complete, when we consider one without the other, even though we be able by abstraction, to have the idea of a mountain or of a place which goes on climbing from bottom to top, without considering that we can also descend by the same from top to bottom. So we can say that it implies contradiction that there are atoms (or parts of matter which have extension and yet are indivisible) because one cannnot have the idea of an extended thing and not have the idea of half of it or a third of it, and consequently not conceive it as divisible into two or three. For, from the sole fact that I consider the two halves of a part of matter, however small it may be, as two complete substances, and the ideas of them have not been rendered inadequate by an abstraction of the mind, I conclude certainly that they are really divisible. And if one says to me that, notwithstanding that I can conceive them, I do not know for all that whether God has not united or joined them together by a connection so tight that they are entirely inseparable and that thus I have no reason to deny this, I shall reply that about any connection by which God can have joined them, I am assured that He can likewise disjoin them, so that, absolutely speaking, I am right in calling them divisible, since He has given me the faculty of conceiving them as such. And I say exactly the same thing about soul and body, and, in general, about all things of which we have diverse and complete ideas, namely, that it implies a contradiction that they are inseparable. But I do not deny, in spite of what I have just said, that there may be many properties in the soul or in the body of which I have no ideas. I deny only that there is any property which is inconsistent with the ideas I have of them, and among others, with the idea I have of their distinction; for otherwise God would be a deceiver and we would have no rule to assure us of the truth.[24]

Thus Descartes' confidence that mind and body are really distinct rests on the conviction (1) that he has ideas of each as a complete being, so that when he thinks of both together he can, without contradiction, suppose that either exists and the other does not exist; (2) that the veracity of God guarantees that what can be thus thought as existing apart without contradiction can exist apart; and (3) that the omnipotence of God can effect the separation.

This, then, is the first argument for the real distinction of mind and body: that it is certain that they can exist apart from one another. The second argument is to the effect that the attributes of thought and extension cannot co-exist in one substance. This argument is sketched in the *Synopsis* of the *Meditations*: "Idemque etiam in ipsa comfirmari ex eo quod nullum corpus nisi divisibile intellegamus, contra autem nullam mentem nisi indivisibilem . . . ; a deo ut eorum naturae non modo diversae, sed etiam quodammodo contrariae agnoscantur."[25] "There is a great difference between mind and body in that body is by nature always divisible and mind is entirely indivisible . . . and this would be sufficient to teach me that the mind or soul of man is entirely different from the body, if I had not already learned it from other sources."[26] Although this argument, like the other one, requires the divine guarantee, it is otherwise independent of the one we have just examined. Descartes has expressly said this. But it can be shown that historically it has an independent source.

Aristotle held that "the mind is not continuous as is a physical magnitude, but it is either indivisible or at any rate is not continuous as is a magnitude. For, if it is a magnitude, how will it think with any one of its parts?"[27] This argument was elaborated by Themistius[28] and Philoponus[29] and eventually found its way into Avicenna's

24. 19 January 1642, *Descartes Oeuvres et Lettres*, pp. 1140-42.
25. *AT*, VII, 13, 19-25; *HR*, I, 141.
26. Meditation vi, *AT*, VII, 85, 86, *HR*, I, 196.
27. *De Anima,* i, 4, 407^{a}6 ff.
28. Ibid., 20.38; 21.6.
29. Ibid., 127.2; 22.4; 131.11.

Psychological Treatises.[30] Suggestions of it are also to be found in Plotinus[31] in a series of proofs that the soul is not the body, and in Proclus.[32]

Descartes had access to the doctrine of the indivisibility of the mind from Augustine,[33] from Aquinas (*Commentary on De Anima*), from Bonaventure (*Sent.*, V, d. 17, a. 1 and 5), from Scotus (*Opus Oxoniense*, ii, d. 3, 11. 6, 8; i, d. 2, q. 7, n. 40), or from the *Commentary* on the *De Anima* of the College of Coimbre (Conimbricenses, *De Anima*, 2, 18, 1 and 3). This is sufficient to show that Descartes almost certainly received this doctrine from his reading and from the lectures he heard as a student at La Fleche.

He often alludes to the incompatibility of thought and extension, considered as principal attributes of substances. Thus in the conversation with Burman, while elucidating the first argument, Descartes stated that "if you clearly conceive corporeal substance, and also clearly conceive thinking substance which is distinct from corporeal substance and which denies it, just as corporeal substance denies thinking substance, you would surely proceed against your faculty of thought and in a very absurd way if you were to say that these two are the same substance, one of which not only does not involve the other but even negates it."[34]

As I said, both arguments depend for their definitive certainty on the divine guarantee. The first argument, namely, that mind and body can exist apart, should be compared with the proof for the external world of matter which is introduced a little later in the sixth Meditation. In the argument for the external world, Descartes urges that God would be a deceiver if either I unconsciously produce my involuntarily received perception or God himself or one of his angelic creatures did so, because ". . . He has given me no faculty to recognize that this is the case, but, on the other hand, a very great

30. *Avicenna's Psychology*, an English translation of Kitāb al-Najāt, Bk. II, ch. VI, by F. Rahman (London: Oxford University Press, 1952), chs. 9, 15. See esp. pp. 46-48, 65-66.

31. *Enneads,* ix, vii.

32. *Commentary on Euclid,* quoted in Philip Merlan, *From Platonism to Neoplatonism,* (The Hague, 1953), p. 19.

33. *De Anima et Ejus Origine,* iv, 21, 25.

34. *AT,* V, 1963.

inclination to believe that they are conveyed to me by corporeal objects."[35] Now, in the letter to P. Gibieuf he tells us that God has given us the faculty to recognize the possibility that mind and body can exist separately or that thought and extension do not involve one another, so that God would be a deceiver if the exercise of this faculty were so to mislead us.

The foregoing is by no means all that can be said about the real distinction of soul and body nor about whether thought is the essence of myself as Descartes conceives these notions. We now know that there are radically different ways of considering mental and physical events. The criticisms of Hume and Kant and the attempts to capture consciousness as a relational complex are all more or less familiar. Moreover, it is certainly open to question whether there are the pervasive qualities of consciousness and extension of which Descartes is so certain. The various arguments for the existence of God used by Descartes or others have been questioned or rejected by many of the philosophers who have come after Descartes. It is not too much to say that the entire foundation of Descartes' system has crumbled. What I have attempted here is only to show how one argument within that system is to be interpreted and how the other parts of Descartes' system support it.

Some recent articles on Descartes have sought to discover some hidden or perhaps even unconscious premises used by Descartes to buttress his distinction and to establish that the essence of the self is thought. But not only is it in the nature of the case impossible to psychoanalyze the dead, it is also not necessary. Descartes has explained in his terms why he held that mind and body are distinct. We may reject his premises as false, or worse, as muddled. We may question the validity of his inferences. But only after a more searching study of Descartes has been made than is obvious from recent articles on the subject can it be established that he needed and used unaknowledged or unavowed premises.

35. *HR*, I, 191.

7

The Sources and Nature of Descartes' *Cogito*

Whether the Delphic maxim "know thyself" can be accomplished in the sessions of silent thought by the solitary thinker is a question which would most probably be given a negative answer by the majority of psychologists of our time. Moreover, whether much self-recognition is philosophically worthwhile might well be denied by a working majority of our philosophical contemporaries. Yet it was such questions which occupied philosophers from antiquity to the beginnings of modern philosophy, and Descartes is particularly known for the answers he provided for both questions.

The *cogito* formula does not occur in Descartes' principal work on metaphysics but in the *Discourse on Method* and *The Search for Truth*, though there are similar formulae in the second and third Meditations. It must be noted that in order to be sure about a correct interpretation of these formulae we must have some idea of the main points which are at issue. These seem to me to be two: the occurrence of self-consciousness and the discernment of a necessary connection between any instance of self-consciousness and the existence of the self-consciousness conceived as a substance. It is necessary, therefore, to examine the history of the idea of self-consciousness as it developed in philosophy from antiquity until the time of

83

Descartes. And it will also be useful to see what the discernment of necessary connection meant to the predecessors of Descartes.

The notion of self-consciousness is difficult to discern in the philosophers of the pre-Socratic period, unless we suppose that we can catch a glimpse of it in one of the fragments of Parmenides the meaning of which is obscure. We are on much firmer ground if we begin with the writings of Plato, including one of doubtful authenticity. In an early dialogue, *Charmides*, serious doubts are introduced concerning both the possibility and the utility of a knowledge of knowledge. In the *First Alcibiades*, however, the capacity of the soul to contemplate the highest part of itself is positively asserted. As this dialogue (whatever its authenticity) was later used by Neoplatonists as a sort of introduction of Plato, it is worth mention in this connection, for it was from Plotinus that the doctrine of self-consciousness, which plays so profound a role in early modern philosophy, was derived. But Plato himself contributed other doctrines which, it seems to me, lead in a different direction. One of these was the argument for the existence of the soul as an explanation of our capacity to grasp many distinct proper sensibles together as well as our capacity to see that each of these sensibles is different from the others and the same as itself, etc., as well as to conceive non-sensibles such as unity and plurality, existence, and the like.[1] This argument has the same general form as Aristotle's argument for the existence of a common sense and may even have been the source of Aristotle's reflections (for there is some evidence that Aristotle borrowed some ideas from the *Theaetetus*, e.g. in *Metaphysics*, Gamma). Now the structure of this argument is from observed effects to an unobserved cause, the characteristic argument which Aristotle used to infer powers from operations.

Thus, though the *First Alcibiades* seems to suggest the possibility of direct self-knowledge, the *Theaetetus* appears to be one of the first arguments to show that indirect inference to the existence of the soul from observed facts of cognition is the correct route to take. It is not impossible for a philosopher, for example Berkeley,[2] to maintain that both are possible. However, the doctrine of the self-

1. *Theaetetus*, pp. 184-86.
2. In the *Principles of Human Knowledge* he holds that we have a notion of self. In the third of the *Dialogues between Hylas and Philonous*, he uses the indirect argument.

cognition of the soul has a complex evolution which splits into two branches. One branch goes directly from Aristotle and culminates in the doctrines of thirteenth-century Scholastics in Christendom, of whom St. Thomas Aquinas is a characteristic example. The other comes from Plotinus and is represented first by Augustine (whose source here is almost certainly Plotinus), and later by a series of philosopher-theologians from Scotus Eriugena through several twelfth-century figures, and by many of the Franciscans of the thirteenth century. The writers of the first branch hold generally that knowledge of the existence and nature of the soul is indirect and that the direct and reflexive acts of the soul are distinct acts. Those of the second maintain, with Augustine, that there is direct self-consciousness and, by implication or explicitly, that the soul knows itself by a single reflexive act. It is important to mention that another development from the second branch is to be found in the philosophers of Islam, especially Avicenna and others influenced by him, and it is significant that the same ultimate source for these Islamic philosophers is also Plotinus and perhaps also Proclus.

It is true that Aristotle (and, we should add, his faithful commentator, Alexander of Aphrodisias) speak of a sensation of sensation by means of which everyone is conscious of his perceiving, but this faculty seems to be confined to the common sense.[3] But there seems no trace of a theory of direct self-consciousness of the soul by itself. On the other hand, there is a doctrine in Aristotle which, when suitably adapted to other purposes, leads almost directly to the Plotinian doctrine. This is the view Aristotle takes, in *Metaphysics*, Lambda, about the activity of the Prime Mover. Here we are told that the divine activity consists of the knowing of knowing; that is, that God's eternal activity is a knowing of His own knowing.[4] Another important clue to what is meant by this doctrine is to be found in *De Anima*, Gamma (4, 432^{a}2), where it is stated that in beings free of matter, mind and its object are identical. This does not necessarily mean that the Agent Intellect is the same as God, and most surely does not mean that each man has his own Agent Intellect and so is capable of self-conscious apprehension. But it is almost certainly the

3. *Ethica Nicomachea* 1170a, 29ff., *De Somno* 2, 455a16, cf. Alexander, p. 148 Wendland, all quoted by H.-R. Schwyzer in *Fondation Hardt*, V, 361-63.
4. 1074^{b}35–1075^{a}4.

historical source of the Neoplatonic doctrine which leads eventually to the view of St. Augustine. However, while Aristotle attributes identity of knower, knowing, and object known to the Agent Intellect and to God, he has no view of direct cognition of a self by self. Instead, the knowledge of the soul is a different thing from knowing that the soul exists or that it is having sensations, etc.

The view of Plotinus, as Schyzer, Merlan, and others have made out convincingly, has its predecessors in Albinus and Apuleius and perhaps others. These are of secondary interest here, because it is the full doctrine of Plotinus that evidently influenced Augustine and Avicenna.

By adopting and adapting the Aristotelian description of the identity of knower and known in matterless Form, and ascribing this to the Second Hypostasis, the Nous, Plotinus was able to perfect the notion of self-consciousness. It is true that souls do not, of themselves, possess this capacity, but they can possess it by becoming, in their return to their source, identical with Nous, and so can enjoy the self-consciousness which is the peculiar feature of Nous. Thus self-consciousness is the self-identity, in Nous, of knower and the known.

In Proclus, who wrote much later than Plotinus, we find essentially the same doctrine. In Proposition 85 of his *Elements of Theology*, the self-recursive character of the self-knowing is described as the unity of knower and known. The same doctrine, then, was available to Augustine in Victorinus' translation of Plotinus, and to the Muslim philosophers through the *Liber de Causis* (dependent on Proclus) and the *Theologia Aristotelis* (derived from Plotinus' *Enneads*, iv-vi).

As a Christian, St. Augustine had to be very selective in what he felt at liberty to derive from Neoplatonic (or other pagan) writers. But it is clear that he adapted the Plotinian doctrine of self-consciousness to his own purposes. These purposes included the need for a direct knowledge which the soul has of itself and a means of refuting the Academic sceptics.

The statement of the first is most clearly stated in *De Trinitate* (Bk. xiv, chap. 6): "... does the mind, then, by one part of itself see another part of itself when it sees itself by thinking, as with some of our members, the eyes, we see our other member which can be in our sight? . . . When the truth is consulted it does not give any of these answers. . . . It remains, therefore, that its sight is something belonging to its nature, and the mind is recalled to it when it thinks of itself, not as it were by a movement in space, but by an incorporeal conversion." As the remainder of the passage reveals, the mind does not always think directly of itself, and this addition differentiates Augustine's view from some others which follow in Augustine's footsteps and for which every consciousness is self-consciousness. There are several statements of Augustine's famous anticipation of the *Cogito* of which perhaps the clearest is *De Civitate Dei*, xi, 26, "Si fallor, sum. . . ." ("If I am deceived, I am; for he who is not cannot be deceived, and therefore if I am deceived, I am.") None of the variant forms of the argument in *De Trinitate*, xv, 12, 21, *De Libero Arbitrio*, ii, 3, 7, *Contra Academicos*, iii, 9, 19, *De Beata Vita*, ii, 2, 7, and *Soliloquies*, ii, 1, 1, state the argument better or as well. It is no wonder that several of Descartes' correspondents called his attention to the remarkable similarities between Augustine's *Cogito* and his own.

The uses to which Augustine's *Cogito* were put by earlier medieval writers such as Scotus Eriugena (in *De Divisione Naturae*, I, 50, p. 27) or Hugo of St. Victor (*Didascallion*, VII, 7; *De Sacramento*, I, pt. 3, VII) are of little interest save to suggest that Augustine's argument was never again lost sight of in Latin Christendom. However, it will be worth attention to examine later on the clash between the Augustinian and Aristotelian views of self-knowledge when both traditions were well-established in the thirteenth and fourteenth centuries. One of the best representations of this opposition can be found in Matthew of Aquasparta, and another in Vital du Four. But before turning to this, it will be interesting to see another line of development in the Islamic world.

It is plausible to assume that Avicenna's general prototype for his famous "flying-man" version of the *Cogito* argument is to be found in the Neoplatonic literature available in the Islamic world of his time. But the special features of his argument resemble very closely an essay of Galen which survives in an Arabic translation. Whatever its origin, however, it has two features which deserve special mention in connection with the Cartesian argument. Firstly, it depends on the occurrence of a knowing of the soul by means of itself, and secondly, it contains a prototype of Descartes' real distinction between mind and body. Avicenna was evidently pleased with the argument because it occurs in several of his writings—in his *De Anima*, his *Isaret*, and in his *Letter on the Resurrection*—and in essentially the same form. As Gilson has shown, the Latin translation of Avicenna's *De Anima* had a decisive influence on medieval writers in the Augustinian tradition.

We have, then, on one side two widely different developments of the Neoplatonic doctrine of self-knowledge and the related argument "I think, therefore I am" converging in the thirteenth-century Latin Christian world, and on the other side, an Aristotelian tradition in which the existence and nature of the soul can be obtained only by an indirect regressive inference. The opposition of these viewpoints can best be exhibited by the views of Aquinas for the Aristotelian side and of Matthew of Aquasparta and Vital du Four for the Augustinian.

According to St. Thomas, the soul knows itself through and by means of knowing its acts. Intellects always in act and actual by their own essences know themselves by these actual essences. But, as the human mind is actualized by the species abstracted from sensible objects, it must first be thus actualized before it can apprehend its own acts. When it does apprehend its own acts, it can be said to perceive itself by itself, but this is indirect and not an immediate self-consciousness without any intermediary.[5] Thus Aquinas seems to be in direct opposition to Augustine and Avicenna on this crucial point.

Among the fourteenth-century theologians, there were a number of advocates of the doctrine that self-knowledge is direct. Nicolas of Autrecourt, for example, in a tract on whether the created intellect can be naturally increased by the word, held that it is possible that every cognition is a cognition of itself, because it may well be the case that the mind has no other act. Ockham, on the other hand, seems to oppose this view in his *Quodlibetal Questions*, since he maintains that the direct and reflex acts are always distinct. Nonetheless, Ockham, and Scotus before him, maintained that knowledge of my own psychic experience is unqualifiedly evident and intuitive knowledge. As for the *Cogito* argument itself, a detailed and acute statement of it can be found in John of Mirecourt.

5. *Summa Theologiae*, Part I, q. 87, a. 1 and a. 3.

Renaissance anticipations of arguments like the *Cogito* are to be found in Campanella and other Renaissance philosophers, and in point of actual publication Silhon anticipated Descartes in the seventeenth-century revival of the argument; but it is very probable that he received it from Descartes.

Enough has been said about the theory of self-consciousness, which was thoroughly developed in Augustinian ways down through the fourteenth century and to which Descartes must, in some form or other, have been exposed. It is now time to turn to the *Cogito* argument itself. I shall contend that it depends on two main points: (1) that the self takes direct cognizance of its own activity, and (2) that it consists of a discernment of a necessary connection between thought (i.e., awareness) and existence. It is, as I believe, the simultaneous affirmation of self-awareness and its connection with existence. As such, it can be regarded as an immediate inference.

Descartes, it must be admitted, stated many different and at first glance inconsistent things about the *Cogito*. In the *Reply to the Second Set of Objections*, he denies that it is a scientific proposition deduced syllogistically from premises more certain than itself. But in the *Principles*, I, 10, he expounds it in a different way which at first sight suggests that it is an inference from premises better known than itself. All this is puzzling, and the conversation with Burman does not completely clear the matter up to everyone's satisfaction. For in the *Conversation with Burman*, as well as in *Principles*, I, 10, Descartes seems to say that the general principle that "whatever thinks exists" is implicit. The difficulties here have, I believe, been sufficiently cleared up by the discoveries of modern formal logic, but in the early and middle seventeenth century, logical questions such as the one here involved were not very well understood. For one thing, it would be anachronistic in the extreme to suggest (as Heinrich Scholz and others have done) that the argument could be rendered as φa; therefore $(\exists x)\varphi x \cdot x = a$. For, first, the idea of quantifiers was not understood until the second half of the nineteenth century. And second, we still have to decide whether or not a is a genuine or only a dummy constant. So Descartes' puzzlement as to what to say is, at the least, understandable. In my own opinion he viewed the matter in an entirely different light. From the *Rules* (especially Rule XII), we learn that there is a necessary connection of the simple

natures of thought and existence. Although the term *simple nature* is
dropped in the *Meditations*, the *Principles*, etc., its place is taken by
other terms, such as *simple properties*, etc. So I think we can safely
assume that the *Cogito* is the simultaneous discernment of the connection of these simple natures, thought and existence, and the
direct cognition of thought by means of itself. If we wanted to
formulate this more exactly, we would have to say that it consists of
the *I think* and *My thought and my existence are necessarily connected* simultaneously apprehended. That more than one thing can
be comprised in one total thought is emphasized by Descartes in the
Conversation with Burman, so the objection which might be raised
by the Schoolmen has been dealt with at least to Descartes' satisfaction. We might say, then, that the *Cogito* is at once a reflexive discernment of thought by itself and an immediate inference of existence
by way of the discernment of a necessary connection between this
case of thought and this case of existence.

That I am a thinking thing (i.e., a substance) is often criticized as
a further inference which is not justified by anything Descartes has
established in the *Cogito*. It must be admitted that in his reply to
Hobbes Descartes makes remarks which encourage this view. But a
closer inspection will show that the question is more complicated.
Descartes, it is true, appeals to the maxim that a property must be a
property of something, and then suggests that there is a further
inference from the *I think* to *I am a thinking thing*. But Descartes
has a view of the relation between attribute and substance different
from his predecessors'. There is only, he says in the *Principles*, a
distinction of reason between any substance and its principal attribute. So we cannot view this further inference in the same light as
we should if it had been made by one of the Schoolmen. If there is
an important movement of thought, it is from any specific occurrence (i.e., any mode) of thought to the attribute itself, rather than
an inference from an accident to a substantial support which is itself
not directly accessible to direct conscious inspection. For Descartes,
the self reveals its principal attribute directly, and so its substantial
nature. Hence, in an important sense, the Cartesian *Sum res cogitans*
differs in meaning from the Scholastic view, insofar as it is not an
inference from an accident which is known to a not directly know-
able substance which supports such an accident in being.

That the *Cogito* is some kind of inference, albeit not expressly syllogistic, is made very clear by Descartes. The presence of *ergo* shows this. This is not to say, however, that Descartes is wholly clear about the difference between an inference schema and the corresponding conditional proposition. But, for that matter, neither were all the Scholastic logicians. Whatever necessary connection meant to the members of the Lyceum, some of the Megaric-Stoic logicians seem to have had the idea that the conditional proposition is true, provided that its antecedent is incompatible with the denial of its consequent. This meaning is, almost without exception, accepted by the logicians of the twelfth century, nor have I discovered any exceptions in the writings of fourteenth-century authorities. Moreover, I have no doubt that this is essentially Descartes' meaning. The evidence can be found by consulting Descartes' writings, especially the *Regulae*, where an explicit definition of *conjunctio* or *connexio necessaria* is to be found.

8

Hume's Theory of Causal Belief

Hume's account of causal belief is a theory in the sense of a kind of scientific hypothesis which *explains* previously given facts and which purports to *predict* other facts. That this is true can be gathered both from the introduction and subtitle of the *Treatise* ("an Attempt to introduce the experimental Method of Reasoning into Moral Subjects") and from a passage of the *Enquiry Concerning Human Understanding*, Sec. 4, Pt. 1, par. 12: "It is confessed, that the utmost effort of human reason is to reduce the principles, productive of natural phenomena, to a greater simplicity, and to resolve the many particular effects into a few general causes, by means of reasonings from analogy, experience, and observation." Both suggest that Hume, like Locke before him, was anxious to apply methods of observation and experiment to the phenomena of consciousness which "the incomparable Mr. Newton" had so successfully applied to physical phenomena. Hume's very words indicate that he had passages of the *Principia* in mind. Like the author of the *Principia*, Hume will not deal with ultimate causes, these being for him unknowable in principle, but will restrict his hypothesis to phenomena, i.e., to facts that are in principle available for inspection. Since the impressions of sensation, according to Hume, arise from such unknown causes, the hypotheses will not deal with them at all. This leaves the task of

92

explaining how ideas and impressions of reflection occur. Impressions of reflection are original existences, it is true. But they arise, according to Hume, after certain impressions of sensation have occurred, and hence general causal laws concerning them are in principle a possible result of observation and experiment. Hume's account of causal belief, like his account of belief in "body," is an attempt to formulate and establish general causal laws about the occurrence of impressions of reflection as dependent on impressions of sensation and as connected with ideas. Therefore, it is as a set of hypotheses or putative "laws of mind" that this account is to be regarded and, ultimately, to be judged.

At the outset it is well to observe, as does H. H. Price,[1] that if we want to learn something valuable from Hume we ought to be prepared to treat him with the same leniency that we treat Kant or, say, one of our own contemporaries. After having pointed out the several absurdities which a literal reading of his text have yielded, and after pointing out the irritating and incredible looseness of language, we ought to try to find out what he was driving at. This will involve in several places a restatement, or better, a reconstruction, of Hume's views. It is to be granted that such a task is far different from that of critical exegesis. And, if it is urged that the results of such reconstruction are commentaries on *their* authors rather than on Hume, my only reply is *non curo*. Philosophical progress largely consists of enlarging, refining, and improving the work of preceding thinkers, and it is at once a tribute to their greatness and our honest modesty that we should thus proceed. Medieval thought, though highly original in many instances, was yet a reconstruction of Plato and Aristotle, and modern thought has been largely a reconstruction of such philosophers as Hume and Kant.

Hume—it must be said in all justice to him—was first of all acutely aware of the defects of his terminology, and he both apologized for it and indicated means of avoiding its misleading connotations. Secondly, when he saw that his views were inadequate or in error he attempted to restate them when he felt this was possible and frankly expressed dissatisfaction when he felt it was not.[2] We must keep

1. *Hume's Theory of the External World* (Oxford, 1940), Introduction.
2. See, for example, the Appendix to the *Treatise of Human Nature*, first part and final remark.

these points in mind when we study Hume's theories about human nature. Of course, Hume does make some serious mistakes and blunders which have nothing to do with terminology. And he contradicts himself in ways that cannot be accounted for wholly in terms of terminological ambiguity. He is sometimes downright confused. Still, if we can overcome some of his difficulties, we may find that a great deal of his theory of causal belief will survive criticism.

II

It can, I think, be conclusively established that the views of cause and cognition of cause to which Hume was opposed were almost universally accepted in Western philosophy from the pre-Socratics down to Hume's own time. The "occasionalists" of Islam and of the seventeenth century are no exception to this. And while Locke saw the impossibility of proving particular causal laws and Berkeley remarked the lack of any necessary connection of sense-given qualities, both philosophers are plainly convinced of the truth and evident character of *some* causal maxims. The object of Hume's attack was not a straw target but an almost universally accepted conviction that there are necessary connections among some distinct events in the world. This necessary connection was conceived to be of a logical character, that is, it was held that the denial of propositions formulating and expressing the connections in question would yield self-contradictions. It was the opinion of Immanuel Kant that Hume showed conclusively that all the arguments that had ever been offered to show the logical (analytic) necessity of causal principles were cases of *Petitio principii* or *ignoratio elenchi*. I entirely agree with this eminent authority on this point and will say no more about it here except for three terminal observations. First, the dialectic of contraries adopted by Hegelians and some British Idealists "answers" Hume by an explicit rejection of the only logic which I can understand let alone accept. Second, I do not know of any authors who hold causal connection to be a relation which, if observed, does not yield knowledge or at least probability about the as yet unexamined cases. Finally, it is a mistake to say that Hume showed only that causality and causation are not known to be logically certifiable. He showed that they were known not to be logically certifiable (in the only sense of certification that is relevant to the issues *he* was concerned with).

III

I shall be concerned here with Hume's theory of causal belief. In the first sense in which Hume defines *cause*, he does not doubt that there are causes. Indeed, it is a well known defect of his arguments concerning liberty and necessity and concerning miracles that he clings too tenaciously to the belief in universal determinism. It is surely a curious charge that Hume denied or doubted causality or causation in the face of this well-known fact. It is his firm belief in the unexceptional regularities of experience that leads him to suppose that an account of the origin and nature of causal belief is possible. For if the imagination, as well as the senses, operates according to regular routines, and if imaginative processes are in principle inspectable, a science of human nature *is* possible. Otherwise, Hume would have held that it was impossible. Hume, then, certainly accepts the principles of causality and causation.[3]

His theory of causal belief is based on two sets of observations. First of all, he is unable to find in the sequence of perceived qualities anything but this: a quality (or group of qualities or pattern of qualities) occurs just before and spatio-temporally contiguous with another quality (or group or pattern of qualities). This sometimes is repeated over and over again. Let us avail ourselves of the convenient and precise notation of *Principia Mathematica*. Let A be one quality and B the other, let P abbreviate *Precedes and contiguous with.* Then what is sense-given is

$$Ax_1 \cdot x_1 Py_1 \cdot By_1$$

$$Ax_2 \cdot x_2 Py_2 \cdot By_2$$

$$\ldots \ldots \ldots \ldots \ldots$$

$$Ax_n \cdot x_n Py_n \cdot By_n$$

3. See *Treatise,* Book I, Part 3, Section 14.

But in the second place, he finds that everyone feels, and in a sense perceives, that there is more involved. For Hume (as for Whitehead), perception "in the mode of presentational immediacy" is the exception, not the rule. Generally, human beings, wise and foolish, learned and vulgar alike, perceive antecedent events as necessarily connected with immediately subsequent events.[4] At first sight, these two observations appear to be inconsistent with one another, and it seems downright perverse to ascribe them to Hume. But those who take the pains to read Book I of the *Treatise* through (without Green's or any other commentary as visual aids) will find that this is what Hume is saying.

4. The mnemonic record of all this would, of course, be

$$(\exists x)(\exists y) \ (Ax \cdot xPy \cdot By)$$
$$(\exists z)(\exists w) \ (Az \sim zPw \cdot Bw)$$

etc.

Observations:

i. I need not be told that A, B are universals and that Hume's nominalism does not permit this. His theory of resemblance and of abstract ideas insists upon it, with the proviso that the universal terms do not refer to anything peculiar and proper to themselves.

ii. Hume speaks of contiguity, and his objectors will be quick to seize upon this and insist on *continuity*. As I remarked before, the objectors do not tell us what they mean by continuity. But I assume that they mean temporal continuity at most. For if they mean qualitative continuity, there are three things to be said:

a. Even if the qualitative continuity is the sheer and exact resemblance of any preceding segment, the temporal difference between the earlier and later parts of the continuum give *different* events or *different* parts of a given event.

b. There are undoubted cases of what would be called causal sequences in which there is a qualitative *discontinuity* however much temporal continuity there may be. It is chiefly the contribution of qualitative discontinuity and temporal continuity which enables us to distinguish cause from effect as to characteristic and to relate cause and effect with respect to space and time.

c. When you have temporal and qualitative continuity you have, I suppose, two phases of a continuant rather than the relation of cause and effect.

See *Treatise,* I, 3, 14. See also *Enquiry Concerning Human Understanding,* sec. 7, pt. 2, last footnote: ". . . and as we *feel* a customary connection between the ideas, we transfer that feeling to the objects; as nothing is more usual than to apply to external bodies every internal sensation, which they occasion."

Such an extravagant claim requires proof, after all we have heard about Hume's psychological atomism. In the first place, Hume does say that impressions and ideas are all distinguishable and therefore separable and therefore capable of separate existence. But he is equally explicit in saying that impressions and ideas are not separated. Only in rare cases of mere reverie or fancy are ideas separated. The rule is that impressions of sensation accompany other impressions of sensation, and that ideas are *associated* with impressions and with other ideas. There may be much that is wrong about all this and many other things which Hume says. But he does say all these things. Well, suppose we grant that. How can the statement that contiguity and sequence is all that is sense-given be reconciled with the statement that in ordinary perception we always have the sense-given supplemented by imagination and supplemented imaginatively in such a way that we do not notice the fact?[5] Hume does not wish, surely, to put upon us with such an outrageous paradox?

I do not find the paradox which may others boggle at here. It is possible to hold that, genetically, we first have

$$Ax_1 \cdot x_1 Py_1 \cdot By_1$$
$$Ax_2 \cdot x_2 Py_2 \cdot By_2$$

and later on we have

$$Ax_n \cdot x_n P\underline{B}_3 \cdot x_n Py_n \cdot By_n$$

(where $\underline{B}$ is a lively idea closely resembling B); whereas, in adult life or from early youth, we have no recollection of the earlier phases of genesis of the great majority of our causal beliefs. And if this account is substantially correct, the sense-given contribution, originally distinct from the imaginative supplement, is distinguishable from it now only by careful experimental introspection. This brings us to the main questions: (1) Is not the separation of sense elements and imaginative elements out of the present perception a vicious abstraction? (2) If not, at any rate, is not this search for atomic parts of a perception a "finding" which is actually making what was not there to begin with at all? That is, does not the search itself produce the

5. *Imagination* is a *terminus technicus* of Hume's *theory*. As Price has remarked, it resembles Kant's productive imagination very closely.

buried treasure which is finally unearthed? (3) What evidence could support such an hypothesis?

I shall not dwell long on the first of these questions. This is the pose of the Absolute Idealists and I think they have been sufficiently answered. Sometimes the questioner assumes a theory of sentience and thought derived from Hegelian or Bradleian idealism. This is not the place to deal with that issue, but I believe it can be shown that the system of idealism depends on a series of mistakes.

The second question can be translated so that, when its metaphors are replaced by soberer language, it is the empirical question: Is the result of introspective analysis anything like its original subject matter? It is certainly possible that it may never be or that it always be like the original. But the hypothesis which seems initially plausible is that it sometimes is and sometimes is not. In any case, such a matter can only be decided empirically. And this naturally brings us to the third question. What is the evidence that there are first sense-given sequences such as

$$Ax_1 \cdot x_1 Py_1 \cdot By_1$$

$$Ax_2 \cdot x_2 Py_2 \cdot By_2$$

$$. . . . .$$

and later

$$Ax_n \cdot x_n P\underline{B}_3, \cdot x_n Py_n \cdot By_n{}^6$$

where $\underline{B}$, as before, is intended as a lively idea closely resembling B), when we have admitted that, in order to make any observations at all, experience must be and is read in causal and substantial terms?

It must be conceded that Hume wrote the theory of causal belief before he wrote the theory of belief in bodies, and that, as a consequence, he speaks in the first instance as if causal associations were between simple impressions (although it should be noted that his examples are all cases of associations of complex impressions, treated as objects, with other complex impressions, treated as objects), whereas it is plain that causal associations are as between

---

6. Actually, this diagram is not sufficiently complicated; we must include the felt determination of habit.

complex events and other complex events. And there is a fundamental difficulty involved here concerning the *discernment* of temporal sequence. This difficulty had been noticed since antiquity, but no one before Kant had attempted an analysis of it. Change in a sense field, it is held, can be noted only when some parts of successive momentary fields are qualitatively and relationally alike and other parts differ either in quality or relation or both. This account of the matter cannot be stated without assuming that there are unnoticed (and unnoticeable) successions which are repetitions and noticed successions which are not repetitious, and I am not sure whether such a theory can be sustained. However, noting the difficulty which is one for Kant as well as for Hume, we may point out that it does not materially affect the present question. For however sequences may be discerned and granted that sequences are always between a pair of complex impressions, and that in adult life experience is always interpreted causally and substantially, how do we have evidence that sequences believed to be causal were once not believed to be so, and so were read off as sequences merely?

Hume holds that we read felt determination in the sense-given by a kind of pathetic fallacy. The proof that it is a pathetic fallacy is that first, we know that some sequences are at first without felt determination and later acquire it after repetition; second, we know that some sequences have felt determination and later lose it (e.g., when counter-instances destroy belief); third, we know that some people believe in causal laws from ignorance or ignoration of counter-instances which others accept as sequences merely. In other words, there are sequences which are sometimes of the form $Ax{\cdot}xPy{\cdot}By$ and sometimes $Ax{\cdot}xP\underline{B}_3{\cdot}xPy{\cdot}By$. We formulate the following law of mind to cover the known cases of genesis of causal belief and also the unknown cases (past and future): Repetition of sequences of the form $Ax{\cdot}xPy{\cdot}By$ are followed by sequences of the form $Ax{\cdot}xP\underline{B}_3{\cdot}xPy{\cdot}By$ provided there are no sequences of the form $Ax{\cdot}xPy{\cdot}{\sim}By_6$.

Now there are three important known exceptions to this general principle. (1) The "learned" or the "wise" in some cases do not have causal beliefs after such repetitions as $Ax{\cdot}xPy{\cdot}By$. (2) The "vulgar" or the "superstitious" frequently form such beliefs even if there are counter-instances or retain them after experiencing counter-instances.

(3) The "learned" sometimes do not wholly reject a law simply because there are counter-instances.

Does Hume find his law of mind false in the face of all these exceptions? Not at all. He finds that the law may still hold if the proper qualifications are made. The point is that people begin by accepting causal laws simply as a result of mere sequences repeated in previous experience. But then later some people are subject to the influence of general principles as well as to the effect of repetition. What is the result of this? Observation shows that such people form causal beliefs less rapidly after many mere repetitions, but more rapidly after a few repetitions when the repetitions have certain peculiar features.[7] Is Hume justified in doing all this? Is generalization about any subject matter justified by observation and experiment?

Hume, when giving an empirical account of the genesis of causal belief, is accepting the two propositions (a) that some causal beliefs are true, and (b) that in order to discover the true ones we must employ general rules which prevent mistakes. That he accepts these beliefs is accounted for (by Hume) by the fact that he is subject to the kind of law according to which causal beliefs occur in the learned and the wise. There is nothing incoherent in this. There is nothing the least bit absurd in my discovering a principle of psychology which would have to be true in fact in order that I make such discovery. As long as I do not assume, in advance and as an explicit premise of my reasoning, that my reasoning is determined by certain psychological laws, there is nothing illogical or circular in my discovering that my reasoning may be subsumed under the principle which I have discovered by means of its operation. Of course, as Mr. L. Palmieri has pointed out to me, it is strictly illegitimate to assume in advance that certain psychological laws are true, and then to use a theory of inference which can only be verified if these laws are used as explicit premises.

IV

Let us try to state what Hume's view is in its simplest form. People attribute a necessary connection to the relation between a cause and

7. *Treatise*, I, secs. 8, 10, 13; cf. *Enquiry Concerning Human Understanding*, sec. 9, footnote.

its effect. They believe not merely that B's follow A's but that B's must follow A's. How is this belief to be accounted for? The necessary connection is not a logically necessary connection; that is, the proposition $(\exists x)(\exists y)(Ax \cdot xPy)$ does not imply By. It is true that $\breve{P}$"$A \subset B$ implies $(\exists y)By$. But why is $\breve{P}$"$A \subset B$ believed? It is not an analytic proposition, and cannot, therefore, be logically certified.

Introspection reveals the felt necessity or determination. At first, it is as if the ineluctable connection is in the sense-given. But more careful inspection reveals that it is perceived only after mere sequences are revealed. And a careful description of the felt determination reveals that it consists of a lively image of the usual attendant B of the sense-given A.[8] If we who are making these observations change the point of view and notice what we are doing, *we* see that the felt determination is only the regular occurrence of (1) an impression of an A, (2) a lively image of a B, and (3) a B, all in quick succession. This is all that our inspection of a case of felt necessity reveals. It is only a more involved sequence than the simple $Ax \cdot xPy \cdot By$ sort of sequence.

If we, the investigators, believe that this is the character of causal beliefs, we feel compelled to suppose that whenever a certain impression occurs, the lively idea of its usual attendant will follow instantly. This compulsive feeling is a feature of our causal belief in the genesis of causal beliefs of the first order (so to speak) and so is itself a causal belief of second order. If we examine this second-order causal belief we shall find only a succession of impression of an F, a lively idea G, impression of a G. Of course an F is a very complex impression and so is a G. But this is as it should be. In any case, we cannot find any necessity other than felt compulsion, which turns out to be merely another sequence of a more complicated sort.

Now, of course, the plausibility of such a view is enhanced if it can be clearly and precisely expressed, and if, as a consequence, the evidence for or against it can be more perspicuously exhibited.

---

8. To be exact, the notion that ideas (as mere images) are representative of sense-given qualities is absurd. But this is a mistake which is hardly peculiar to Hume. We should say, instead of *the idea of a B*, either *the idea that there is a B*, or *the B-like image*. Images as such can be copies, but they cannot symbolize anything in particular.

Hume's insistence on the importance of general rules in the genesis of scientific belief is on the right lines. But he nowhere, as far as I know, shows in detail how such beliefs arise, nor does he trouble to explain their superiority to the uncriticized beliefs of the vulgar. This is a serious omission, for his own account of causal beliefs, being intended as a reliable hypothesis, must differ plainly both from undisciplined speculation and from vulgar prejudice.

The question is, then, whether it is possible to give such an account within the framework of his theory. The genesis of the habit of using the methods of difference or of concomitant variation is, doubtless, a more complex affair than simple habituation involving the method of agreement. In fact, the method of agreement itself, regarded as a method of rejecting possible *sine qua non* conditions, is a more complicated matter than simple habituation. The defects of Hume's theory begin to show up when we consider this question. In the first place, as we have seen, Hume uncritically assumed that we have, in a causal law, causal characteristics which were *sine qua non* as well as sufficient conditions. And, having made this uncritical assumption, he was able to present a set of general rules which, he thought, exhaust the "logic I think proper to employ in my reasoning." The genesis of these general rules, it must be admitted, would be a relatively easy thing to account for. But unfortunately, the crucial rule here does not follow from either his psychological or his logical definition of cause.

This requires some explanation. If all sufficient conditions are also *sine qua non*, we can infer from the dispensability of a factor that it is insufficient. Hence one clear experiment suffices to establish a causal law, and we do not have to wait upon that repetition from which the *first* idea of causal connection arose.[9] The general rules, far from making us more wary, would induce a specious security. We would, of course, learn to reject certain alleged causes as insufficient or as dispensable factors, and some wariness would, of course, come in this way. But this would be about all. The psychological genesis of these general rules would be easily accounted for. We are first subject to customs of the first order, simple unsuspected

9. *Treatise*, I, 3, 15, "Rules by which to judge of causes and effects," Rules 4 and 5.

repetition. Then we discover that some of these repetitions admit of exception, while others *apparently* do not. Later still, we notice that repetitions which occur with the greatest variety of other circumstances appear to be sustained, while those which occur with less variety are, generally, not sustained by subsequent experience. So we are gradually habituated by a second-order custom, *viz.*, suffering only such first-order customs as also display the variety in question. The habitual inference of the learned thus differs from that of the vulgar by being a second-order custom, the acceptance of first-order customs which, to speak paradoxically, repeatedly display differences rather than likenesses in qualities other than the ones on which the first-order custom may be founded. But, unfortunately, the matter is not only not so simple as this but also has a different direction. The inductions of the learned are, on Hume's own statement, as much in the nature of habitual caution as of acceptance.

The true situation, as it appears to me, is this. There is, if our observations of human behavior can be at all depended upon, a primary tendency to anticipate B given A, provided that previous cases of the A,B sequence have occurred. But there is also a tendency to cease anticipating in this way when B fails, given A, or when B occurs without A. We gradually notice not merely that certain repetitions continue and others do not but that those which do continue have some further features, particularly the capacity to withstand deliberate attempts at refutation.[10] Thereafter, we tend to anticipate on the basis of sequences which have hitherto withstood attempts at refutation.

Now, there is no objection to attributing the primary beliefs to custom. And we can also say with some propriety that the second-order belief just explained is the result of habituation. But the intermediate stages in the formation of these secondary beliefs involves a complicated set of inferences which cannot be called habits or customs with any propriety at all. Hence the general rules which determine the beliefs of the learned can, and do, become habitual. But their genesis is not due to *mere* repetition, and involves logical

10. The peculiar features are, for example, that taken by pairs the sequences exhibit the "figure of difference," and taken by other pairs the sequences exhibit the "figure of agreement."

operations which cannot be construed in terms of habit in Hume's sense. This does not mean, of course, that they admit of no psychological explanation of any kind. On the contrary, it seems plain that since *these* inferences are logically certified, we may suppose there is some relatively simple explanation analogous to the theory of a logical machine. The various parts of the system are, therefore, relatively simple. But the combination of primary habits, formation of simple secondary habits, logical inferences of refutation, and finally the secondary habits of the man of science, all this is a very complicated system.

And if this complicated system represents anything like the true system of the scientist's convictions and practice, Hume's positive theory of causal belief and his negative critique of induction require modification. The positive theory is incomplete as it stands, and requires additions which, as I have argued, go beyond habitual features. The negative critique must be modified in the following ways. Hume argued that the belief in the uniformity of experience is established by habits which are so strong that we believe in causes and effects even where they are not observed. But if the foregoing account of learned caution is sound, the belief in uniformity has a different form for the learned. The unknown instances, we would say, in the great proportion of cases tend to resemble the known cases when the known cases survive the deliberate scrutiny by the methods of agreement, difference, and concomitant variation. We are habituated to believe this on the basis of previous experience. But it is a very complicated sort of habit.

There is a temptation to say that the learned behave differently. It is not that they positively believe that certain generalizations which have been scrutinized are very probably true, but rather that they withhold belief from all that have not passed the scrutiny successfully. But this, I think, is wrong. You cannot withhold belief from certain generalizations unless you are never prepared to believe anything, whatever the situation may be. And so I think that the learned as well as the vulgar are given to beliefs of some kind.

It is important to emphasize that, in any case, some past repetitions are merely the genetic basis for belief. They cannot constitute a logical basis, for there is no logical basis—at any rate, no logical basis for positive convictions that certain universal propositions are true. But there is a logical basis for the *rejection* of beliefs of this kind. And it is this logic of the affair which is of central importance in forming the scientist's convictions, not simply about the truth of particular generalizations but also about the general reliability of experimental induction. The scientist believes that he will often fail if he neglects experiment. He believes he will succeed if he follows experiment. This belief is a kind of induction about induction.

It is now reasonably plain what kind of evidence is needed to substantiate this general theory of causal belief, and also what kind of evidence would refute it. I do not propose to discuss further the question of whether the theory, with my suggested modifications, is tenable in terms of evidence available.

V

I shall now turn my attention to questions closely related to the theory of the genesis of causal beliefs. These questions are concerned with the content of such beliefs. And I shall ask first of all whether Hume correctly formulated the definition of *cause* in what he called the "philosophical" sense of the term.[11] Then I shall be concerned with the general causal principles which, Hume held, lie at the foundation of all experimental reasoning. Finally, I shall ask whether any principles of this sort can reasonably be supposed to lie at the foundation of experimental reasoning.

Hume defines cause (as a philosophical relation) in the following way: x is the cause of y if x precedes and is spatio-temporally contiguous with y and if everything like x is in a like relation to those objects like y. It is clear from what is said about the rules by which to judge of causes and effects that Hume regards all causal connection as reciprocal: i.e., if B's are caused by A's they are only caused by A's.[12] Now this is the first defect in Hume's definition. His theory of causal belief allows us to infer from causes to effects but not

11. Hitherto we have spoken of the "natural" relation of causation. (See *Treatise*, I, 3, 7; cf. I, a, 5.–Eds.)

12. Hume's confusion on this point goes very far; see the *Enquiry Concerning Human Understanding*, where Hume says, "But it is pretended that some causes are necessary, some not necessary." Here Hume confuses his notion of "necessitation of habit" with *sine qua non* condition.

conversely. But his rules permit inference from causes to effects and from effects to causes. Furthermore, the theory of causal belief offers us nothing which is inconsistent with a so-called plurality of causes. And thus Hume's definition includes more than is justified by his previous discussions; neither the theory of causal belief nor the analysis of the sense-given antecedents of a causal belief afford any reason for the definition as it stands. Accordingly, we shall amend it as follows:

$$X_1 \text{ causes } y_1 \text{ =def } (\exists A)(\exists B)Ax_1 \cdot By_1 \cdot X_1 Py_1 \cdot \check{P}``A \supset B$$

There is, however, another serious defect in the definition which Kant has the merit of having discovered. It does not include the irreversibility of causal sequences in contradistinction to the noncausal ones. Accordingly, we shall have to add something which Hume failed to observe, but which as Price noted, is in no way inconsistent with, or requires a fundamental modification of, Hume's philosophy. A sequence xPy is reversible if there is an A and a B which respectively characterize x and y, and xPy, and if $(\exists z)(\exists w)Az \cdot Bw \cdot wPz$. Accordingly we define: x_1 causes y_1 =def $(\exists A)(\exists B)Ax \cdot By \cdot xPy \cdot \check{P}``A \subset B \cdot \check{P}``A \subset \sim B$. So much has been written about Kant's "answer" to Hume that it seems scarcely worth while to add more, but I think the precise expression of concepts which contemporary logic affords will, perhaps, provide some elucidation of the issues.

Kant is supposed to have discovered that successions are successive objectively if it is impossible that they be reversed; otherwise they are subjective. This "impossibility" must be carefully scrutinized. It is supposed on the one hand to distinguish the sequences of subjective appearances from the objective sequences which are intersubjective and on the other hand to distinguish causal from noncausal sequences. Now this simply will not do. The reversible sequences must be reversible for all observers (excepting those who can only look *de haut en bas* either from an excess of snobbery or because of a wry neck), and the irreversible sequences must also be irreversible for all observers (excepting those who believe in final causes and confuse them consistently with efficient ones). Now if this is so, the main distinction is between objectively reversible and objectively irreversible sequences.

With these preliminaries we can proceed to point out that reversibility and irreversibility are concerned essentially with the order of occurrence of qualities, not of events. Hence, successions are presupposed in Kant's as well as Hume's systems which are, and must be, irreversible in some other sense. These are the successions of individual events. The definition of reversible and irreversible sequences makes this quite clear.

x precedes y reversibly =def $\cdot xPy\cdot(\exists z)(\exists w)(z$ like $x\cdot w$ like $y\cdot wPz)$

x precedes y irreversibly =def $\cdot xPy\cdot\sim(\exists z)(\exists w)(z$ like $x\cdot w$ like $y\cdot wPz)$

It is obvious that both kinds of succession require the asymmetrical relation of succession P, which means that no two *individual* events in this relation can be both before and after each other.

Kant's notion of reversible successions is based, of course, on the conviction that the coexistent parts of a physical object can be surveyed in succession-indifferent ways, and that whatever features can be obtained in succession-indifferent ways are coexistent parts. But if this is the case, then the *reversibility of succession* is part of what is meant by a physical object, just as the irreversibility of succession is part of what is meant by a causal connection. In other words, we would refuse to apply *physical object* when some successions were irreversible, and we would refuse to apply the notion of cause when certain successions were reversible. Now this gives us the clue, I believe, to the allegedly nonexperiential origin of the concepts of physical object and causal nexus. These concepts denominate experience-complexes which (up to the present) satisfy certain conditions among which are reversibility in the case of one and irreversibility in the case of the other. Irreversibility *is* a necessary condition of causal nexus just because we would refuse to apply the concept of causal nexus to reversible sequences. The concept of causal nexus is a precondition of experience, in the sense that if we did not accept certain sequences as causal we would not have anything like what we now understand by experience. Yet nothing has been said which precludes the empirical origin of these concepts. Once again it must be insisted, whatever authorities are against us, that there is no inconsistency in holding that (1) we would not, in fact, make the observations necessary to detect the genesis of beliefs unless we have and act upon such beliefs and unless up to the present many of those beliefs have been confirmed by experience, and yet that (2) we have substantial evidence that such beliefs arise empirically and have contents which can be entirely elucidated in terms of undefined descriptive predicates and logical constants. That is, neither the origin of causal and substantial beliefs nor their contents requires us to assume their pre-experiential origin.

When particular experiences fail to satisfy the conditions of causality and physical thinghood we do not conclude that causal nexus does not obtain or that there are no physical things. We still retain these "categories" but refuse to apply them to the experiences in question. I conclude that Kant was perfectly right in what he concluded but gave a wrong account of the genesis and content of the analogies of experience.

There are yet some further difficulties to be cleared up before we can regard Hume's definition as satisfactory. Mill has supplied the means of further correcting Hume's definition, although what Hume says in the *Treatise* and *Enquiry* shows that he was well aware of the needed addition. We must restrict causal generalizations to situations in which "counteracting" cause factors are absent or removed. Now we need only modify our definition by the condition that such interfering conditions are not present. Thus where F = interfering conditions, $\breve{P}``A\text{-}F \subset B$. This takes care of what Mill called the unconditionality of the sequence. The objection may be made that we do not know how extensive or narrow F should be in order to formulate a true causal law. This is an irrelevant objection, because there is no formal way of being sure that a law is true. We make F as extensive or as narrow as the evidence warrants, and that is all we could do on any theory. Hume took all this into account, in his discussion "Liberty and Necessity," for example.

The most curious objection to Hume's theory of the meaning of *cause* has been recently brought in the form of controversy about the meaning of contrary-to-fact conditional. Before I attempt to state this objection, it is well to point out a feature of reconstruction which is frequently overlooked. As an example, there is a widespread supposition that an English statement must be reconstructed in one way: given object statements in English must be replaced by object statements in the language system. This is plainly impossible. *John left because Mary insulted him*, for instance, cannot be reconstructed in this way. For it may be plausibly reconstructed as follows: *If any one insults John he leaves* is true; *Mary insulted John* is true; therefore *John left* is true. And this reconstructs the original statement of the object language in the metalanguage. Now I shall suggest that if we reconstruct contrary-to-fact conditionals in this way, we shall have no difficulty in bringing them into line with Hume's major contentions.

It is true that all that is asserted in a universal conditional (we may, for illustrative purposes, take the simplest form of such statements) is $A \subset B$ which means $\sim(\exists x)(x \epsilon A \cdot x \epsilon \sim B)$ which could be trivially true if $\sim(\exists x)x \epsilon A$. But we always, in fact, assert such conditionals as evidence which means that $(\exists x)x \epsilon A$, and this precludes the trivialization. Now when a man asserts *If this vase were dropped it would break*, he plainly intends to assert two independent statements, independently arrived at, viz., $Vx \cdot Dx \underset{x}{\supset} Bx$ and $Va \cdot \sim Da$. And implicit also is the further assertion $(\exists x)Vx \cdot Dx \cdot Bx$, which constitutes the evidence for the conditional. Hence despite the wide publicity that contrafactual conditionals have received, they do not appear to constitute a real threat to Hume's analysis of causal beliefs.

From all this, it is clear that a contrary-to-fact conditional expresses a belief in two independent propositions. Now one of these is a causal belief, and on Hume's theory such a belief requires at least one illustration in experience. On his terms, then, the paradoxes of formal or material conditionals cannot be constructed. This is the solution of the whole problem of contrary-to-fact conditionals. And it should be reasonably clear that nothing in its solution involves major alterations in Hume's theory.

There are, however, some major difficulties with Hume's doctrines about causal connection to which I now turn my attention. These are concerned with general principles. Hume maintains that the learned, at least, realize that they are assuming the uniformity of nature and the universality of causal connection. If we attempt to formulate these assumptions we encounter difficulties which appear to be insurmountable. I shall attempt to show this by successive approximations. First, let us suppose the term *cause* to be undefined. The principles then are: *(y)(∃x)[x, y* ∈ events ⊃ *x* causes *y]* and *x,y* ∈ events ·*x* causes *y·x'* like *x·y'* like *y·* ⊃ *x'* causes *y'*. Events may be defined as members of the field of the relation *P* (preceding and spatio-temporally contiguous with). We then have (where *C* is the class of events)

(1)   *(y)(x)[x,y*∈*C·xPy·*⊃*x* causes *y]*

This is the principle of causality. The principle of causation is

(2)   *x* causes *y·x'Lx·x'Py'·* ⊃ *·yLy'*

(where *L* means *resembles*).

Now Hume has provided a definition of *cause* so that the principles become

(1)   *(y)(∃x)(∃A)(∃B)[xPy·Ax·By·P̆ "A* ⊂ *B·P̆ "A* ⊂ *~B]*

(2)   *(x)(x')(y)(y')(∃A)(∃B){x,y,x',y'* ∈ *C'P* ⊃ *([xPy·Ax·By·*
         P̆ "A ⊂ *B·P̆ "A* ⊂ *~B]* ⊃ *(Ax'·x'Py'·*⊃ *By')}*

It is obvious that the principle of causation has now become an analytic consequence of the definition of *cause*.

Now it seems that there is another meaning to the principle of causation which is not an analytic consequence of the definition of cause and is closer to what Hume, at times, appears to mean by the uniformity of nature. It is that for every characteristic of events there is a determining characteristic. For Hume certainly supposes that all events have causes and that similar causes have similar effects. He also supposes that the influence of general rules leads us to seek causal explanation for *sorts* of events. Now the natural way to formulate such a rule is to say: For every abstraction-class *B* of events, there is an abstraction-class *A* of events such that the immediate successors of *A*'s are *B*'s (though the immediate predecessors of *A*'s are non-*B*'s) and there is an *A* such that the the immediate predecessors of *B*'s are *A*'s (though the immediate predecessors of *A*'s are non-*B*'s).

Since every event belongs to some abstraction-class, this formula also includes the principle of causality. However, the formula is, as it stands, implausible, indeed, plainly false. There is no reason to suppose that *every* abstraction-class fulfills such a condition. For it is possible that some abstraction-classes are associated with others in a statistical regularity and possible that some may not be regularly associated with others in any way.

Moreover, it is possible that some general principle of this sort might be true of groups of abstraction-classes but not of single ones. As a consequence, the only comprehensive formulas for causal laws appear to be false or doubtful. For we cannot, in advance, know what further conditions to put upon abstraction-classes in order to obtain a true formula. In fact, the change from abstraction-classes of events to *objects* does not help us in this regard. We have many qualitative laws, but we do not know any characteristics common to all determined characters which enable us to state a general formula which has any plausibility. What is the common feature of all antecedents and all consequents in the qualitative laws which we at present accept? I know of none.

It is sometimes suggested that we introduce quantitative considerations. But this does not make any material difference. As long as we restrict ourselves to empirical quantitative laws, we are in the same situation. The laws do not have common forms. The way in which laws are brought together in a system is by means of a theory. But there are many theories, and as yet no comprehensive one from which all quantitative laws can be deduced.

It is possible that such a theory may be found. But its form will be determined by the previously confirmed laws and subsidiary theories. There is no way to determine, in advance, the form which a comprehensive theory will assume.

9

The Novelty of
Hume's Philosophy

Rochefoucauld said in his ninety-third Maxim that old men delight in giving good advice as a consolation for the fact that they can no longer set bad examples. It was chiefly this which made me resolve against attempting to give you any part of my own philosophy this evening. Instead, I wish to discuss some aspects of Hume's philosophy in its original background. It is my conviction that, among philosophers of the first rank, it was Hume more than any of his contemporaries or prececessors who brought about the transition from a theological to a naturalistic view of the world. Spinoza and others had contributed much to this process. The progress of the natural sciences from the late Renaissance to Newton discredited almost all the alleged physical evidence which had been used to support the medieval view of nature. Social, political, and religious upheavals made it impossible to enforce a common orthodoxy in philosophical essentials. At the same time, however, many features of ancient and medieval metaphysics, transformed to some degree to be sure, were still retained and defended by the majority of thinkers

Presidential address delivered before the Sixty-third Annual Meeting of the Western Division of the American Philosophical Association at the Edgewater Beach Hotel, Chicago, April 29, 30, May 1, 1965, and printed in the *Proceedings and Addresses of the American Philosophical Association*, 38 (1965), 17–35. Reprinted by permission.

of the seventeenth and eighteenth centuries. Hume made the most complete break with this time-honored tradition. In France, there were several who went further than Hume in philosophical radicalism. But they were mostly thinkers of the second rank at the best who had the courage of other men's convictions.

In discussing the novelty of Hume's thought I have been obliged to omit from consideration Hume's contributions to the philosophy of religion and to morality. Fortunately, the first of these subjects has been excellently treated by Norman Kemp Smith[1] and by Antony Flew in *Hume's Philosophy of Belief.*[2] As for the second, the core of Hume's moral doctrines was derived from Francis Hutcheson. Hume argued the case in his own way and certainly had some original points of detail. I do not think that his greatest contributions to modern philosophy occur in this field, despite the fact that it was undoubtedly one of Hume's main interests. There was another reason, aside from limitations of time, which made me diffident about discussing the subject. Many years ago I was persuaded by some of my colleagues not to continue to teach moral philosophy. I am reliably informed that the teaching and practice of morality at my university have noticeably improved since that time.

In the *Abstract* and elsewhere Hume spoke of his *Treatise of Human Nature* as having "such an air of singularity, and novelty as claimed the attention of the public." There has been considerable discussion among scholars about the nature of this novelty. Kemp Smith may be correct in supposing that essentially it was the application to whole ranges of human thought that Hutcheson had proposed, and that Hume had adopted, concerning the foundation of morality.[3] The discovery that custom was the guide of life in causal judgments as well as in moral ones certainly loomed large in Hume's mind in the *Abstract*. There and elsewhere, Hume acknowledges his indebtedness to previous writers on theoretical and practical philosophy, and so we may be sure that he was awaure, to a great extent, of this debt to his predecessors. But the history of the philosophical past was very imperfectly known in Hume's time, and although printed versions of medieval philosophical and theological works were accessible, it is improbable that the youthful Hume would have

1. *The Philosophy of David Hume* (1941; New York, 1966).
2. New York, 1961.
3. Smith, *Hume*, chs. 1 and 2.

spent much time in serious perusal of authors for whom most of the eighteenth century had nothing but contempt. Berkeley had, as an Anglican divine, some acquaintance with the Schoolmen, and even Hobbes had recommended the study of Suarez. Had Hume read diligently some of the Scholastic discussions, he might have seen that some of his discoveries and novelties had been anticipated. As it is a fair assumption that he did not do so, we may fairly credit him with rediscovering and therefore having made a permanent part of moddern philosophy ideas which, in point of fact, had turned up much earlier. Certainly, there is every reason to believe that it was Hume's own insight that exposed the fallacies in the attempt of Hobbes, Locke, and Clarke to prove the principle that whatever has a beginning has a cause. And just as certainly, it was Hume's own idea to substitute custom for logical intuition in the explanation of causal belief. To say all this, however, is not fully to understand Hume's place in the history of Western philosophy. The novelty of Hume has to be seen in the larger historical context of all Western thought.

Accordingly, I propose to survey, of necessity very incompletely, anticipations of some aspects of Hume's thought among ancient and medieval philosophers. This will reveal, at the least, that part of Hume's originality consists in a unique combination of many ideas which had occurred to previous philosophers, whether known to Hume or not. In general, it can be said that while human thought is creative, it is not vouchsafed to men to effect *creatio ex nihilo*.

There is another reason for the study of origins or anticipations of thought. Even when there is little or no likelihood of any direct historical influence, the fact that the same or similar ideas have occurred to thinkers at various periods of time and in vastly different intellectual cultures has some value in the assessment of their soundness. It is sometimes true that earlier statements of an important and valid point are superior in clarity and cogency to later ones. This was especially the case with respect to the logical status of causal principles. It is well known today that Hume had no theory of propositions, and the inadequacies of his psychological theories are notorious. The probability that Hume's principal contentions will survive these deficiencies is enhanced by the fact that some of them were elaborated by philosophers who were at least free from Hume's mistakes in psychology and the radical inadequacies in logic which Professor Zabeeh has so well made out.[4]

HUME'S CRITIQUE OF CAUSALITY AND CAUSATION

I shall adopt the practice of some older writers and refer to the principle that whatever has a beginning has a cause as the principle of causality, and to the principle that like causes have like effects as the principle of causation. The latter principle becomes an analytic proposition after Hume defines the meaning of *cause* in the sections on necessary connection of the *Treatise* and the *Enquiry*, but in the critical parts of the *Treatise* and *Enquiry* it is not, and could be stated as equivalent to the uniformity of nature. I shall be concerned with Hume's criticism of previous views and the extent to which he was anticipated by previous writers on the subject in Western philosophy.

At least one element of this criticism might have been suggested to Hume by several ancient writers. It will be remembered that Hume held, as a result of his successful denial that causality and causation are intuitively or demonstratively certain, that anything can cause anything.[5] This had already been noticed by Epicurus[6] and by Lucretius in *De Rerum Natura*.[7] Hume might have encountered it also in Sextus Empiricus.[8] But the point would have been obscured, because Epicurus and Lucretius use it to establish, by a curious empirical argument, that nothing comes from nothing. Hume might also have learned from Sextus Empiricus[9] that it can be argued that nothing is the cause of anything. Yet there is really nothing in

4. Farhang Zabeeh, *Hume: Precursor of Modern Empiricism* (The Hague, 1960).

5. *Enquiry Concerning Human Understanding*, pt. 4.

6. To Herodotus, in Diogenes Laertius, *Lives of Eminent Philosophers*, x, 38–39, trans. in 2 vols. by R. D. Hicks (1925; Cambridge, Mass., 1950), II, 566–69.

7. I, 125. *De Rerum Natura*, trans. W. H. D. Rouse, The Loeb Classical Library (Cambridge Mass., 1959), pp. 10–20.

8. *Outlines of Pyrrhonism*, Bk. 3, ch. V; trans. R. G. Bury, 3 vols. (London, 1933–36), pp. 337, 345.

9. Ibid., p. 339.

these sources which might have suggested to Hume the main lines of his own critique. It is not impossible, but highly unlikely, that any ancient author anticipated Hume in this connection. Several forms of causal maxims were certainly regarded throughout most of the history of Western philosophy as somehow ineluctably necessary truths.[10] The principle of *Ex nihilo nihil fit* was perhaps first enunciated by Melissus of Samos.[11] Both Empedocles[12] and Anaxagoras[13] seem to agree with the Eleatics in this, and the conviction that nothing occurs without a cause is clearly stated in one of the Hippocratic writings.[14] It is to Plato, however, that we must turn for emphatic statements that whatever comes into being does so necessarily as the result of a cause.[15] Although the Forms may have no need of a cause, everything in the realm of genesis of necessity requires one.

Aristotle states the principle of causality in so many forms that it would be impossible to summarize his statements short of a treatise. If anything is clear, however, it is that change of any kind necessarily requires a cause.[16] It is also clear that Aristotle enunciated a principle something like the uniformity of nature: that the same cause while in the same condition always has the same effect.[17] This principle is qualified to hold only for irrational potentialities.[18] Finally, Aristotle's theory that potentialities are actualized only by actualities ostensibly or otherwise like themselves requires a resemblance between each cause and its effect.[19] It is clear that Aristotle regarded all these principles as necessary in some sense, which seems to be that

10. This conviction occurs early in Eastern philosophy as well. See *The Chandogya Upanishad,* VI, 2, 1; trans. Swami Swahananda, 2nd ed. (Madras, 1965), pp. 415-16.

11. *Die Fragmente der Vorsokratiker,* ed. by Hermann Diels with additions of Walther Kranz, 5th ed. (Berlin, 1934-37), 1B. Cf. Kathleen Freeman, *Ancilla to the Pre-Socratic Philosophers* (Cambridge, Mass., 1962), p. 48.

12. Diels, *Die Fragmente,* 11B, 12; Freeman, *Ancilla,* p. 52.

13. Diels, 11B; Freeman, p. 85.

14. *De Arte,* 6,

15. *Laws,* X, 895; *Philebus,* 26; *Timaeus,* 28A.

16. *Physics,* vii, 1, 241^{b}25; *Metaphysics,* xii, 5, 1071^{b}29-31.

17. *De Generatione et Corruptione,* ii, 10, 336^{a}27-28; *De Caelo,* ii, 13, 295^{a}28; *Physics,* ii, 18, 199^{b}25; *Metaphysics,* ix, 8, 1049^{b}24-25.

18. *Metaphysics,* ix, 2, 1046^{b}5-6, ix, 5, 1048^{a}8.

19. *Metaphysics,* vii, 7, 1032^{a}12; *Physics* viii, 5287^{b}9 ff. 1032^{a}12.

of absolute necessity. That the arguments used to show this have a merely verbal force does not seem to have occurred to any ancient writer.[20]

The Stoics appear to have maintained that the principle of causality is necessary, and that the apparent absence of a cause is really a case of hidden causes.[21] Plotinus[22] explicitly holds that a cause for every actualization is necessary, Augustine[23] similarly holds that every changeable thing requires a cause in something other than itself, and Anselm[24] holds it altogether inconceivable that something exist without a cause.

If we examine the writings of the Muslim philosophers of the Middle Ages we find the same doctrine repeatedly asserted. Alkindi[25] speaks of the principle of causality (what has a beginning has a cause) as something evident. The author of the Gems of Wisdom, probably Avicenna,[26] holds that "whatever exists after not having existed, must be brought into existence by a cause, nothing cannot be a cause of anything," and in writings which are certainly from Avicenna, it is plainly asserted that all beings other than the one in whom essence and existence are identical must derive existence from something else.[27] Moreover, "whatever comes into existence by a cause does so necessarily; it cannot be otherwise."[28]

Among the Muslim theologians of the Asharite persuasion, another and different view of causality was proposed which has been cited

20. Eduard Zeller, *Philosophie der Griechen*, Vol. III, Ab. 2, H. 2.

21. *De Fato*, 574; 7, 572.

22. Book v, Tractate 9, no. 4 of *The Enneads*, trans. Stephen MacKenna, 2nd ed., rev. B. S. Page (London, 1956), p. 436.

23. *De Libero Arbitrio*, ii, ch. 17; *De Trinitate*, ii, ch. 1.

24. *Monologion*, ch. iii.

25. "Liber Al Kindi de Intellectu [et Intellecto]," 17 ff. This work is translated into Latin by A. Nagy in *Beiträge zur Geschichte der Philosophie des Mittelalters*, vol. II, pt. 5 (Münster, 1897).

26. Avicenna (Ibn Sina), *Metaphysica sive Prima Philosophia* (Frankfort am Main, 1966), Tractatus octavi vel octavi libri, Cap. III; cf. *Metaphysices Compendium*, trans. into Latin by Nematallah Carame (Rome, 1926), Tractatus II, Capitulum 3, passim.

27. Ibid., VIII, 3.

28. *Danesh-Nameh*, trans. into French as *Le Livre de science* (The Book of Wisdom) by Mohammed Achenna and Henri Masse, 2 vols. (Paris, 1955), I, 135.

from the time of William Hamilton[29] and Ernest Renan as an anticipation of Hume's doctrines. In the interests of Muslim orthodoxy
these theologians maintain that God is the only cause in the universe and that the apparent causal routines observed in nature are
only the habitual ways in which God acts. The interesting features of
this view are set forth by Al-Ghazali in his refutation of the Muslin
philosophers. Avicenna is the principal but not the only target of his
criticism. There is no logically necessary connection between distinct
finite beings: the affirmation or denial of one of them does not
imply an affirmation or denial of any other. Moreover, though philosophers appeal to observation to establish causal connections in
nature, all that observation reveals is concomitance of two events,
not causal connection. There is no proof that a hidden agent may
not be the cause of every alleged causal nexus in nature.[30]

Thus: "The philosophers have no other proof [that fire burns
cotton] than the observation of the occurrence of the burning, when
there is contact with fire, but observation proves only a simultaneity,
not a causation, and in reality there is no other cause but God."[31]

"[Only the impossible cannot be done by God and] the impossible consists in the simultaneous affirmation and negation of a
thing, or the affirmation of the more particular with the negation of
the more general, or the affirmation of two things with the negation
of one of them."[32]

The verbal character of the arguments used to show that different
things are connected by causal necessity is clearly realized by Al-
Ghazali. Thus to the argument that volition cannot be separated
from what is willed, he says, "by *will* is implied the seeking of something; and if we assume a seeking without knowledge there cannot
be a will, and we would then deny what he had implied."[33] Again,

29. *Lectures on Metaphysics and Logic by Sir William Hamilton*, ed. Rev.
Henry Mansel and John Veitch (Boston, 1860), pp. 541–42.

30. *Tahafut Al-Falasifah*, trans. into English as *The Incoherence of the
Philosophers* by Sabih Ahmad Kamali, Pakistan Philosophical Congress Publication No. 3 (Lahore, 1963), Problem 17, p. 185.

31. *Tahafut Al-Tahafut*, trans. into English as *The Incoherence of the
Incoherence* by Simon van den Berg, 2 vols. (London, 1954), I, 317.

32. Ibid., I, 329.

33. Kamili, trans., *Philosophers*, p. 195.

"It is impossible that in the inorganic knowledge should be created because we understand by inorganic that which does not perceive."[34]

When Averroes attempted to refute Al-Ghazali about eighty years later, he pointed out that the denial of the efficacy of secondary causes removed any possibility of a legitimate proof for the existence of God. This was because Averroes held that only Aristotle's argument in *Physics*, viii has the force of a demonstration. As he put it, "the unseen must always be known by means of what is seen." Averroes held that if we reject secondary causes "we have no argument against those who think that there is no God and that everything has come into being by chance."[35] Finally he urged that the denial of causality would allow that anything could come from anything, a point already made by Epicurus and Sextus Empiricus.[36] As far as is known, Averroes regarded the principle of causality as self-evident, and so neither requiring nor allowing of any proof.[37] Averroes' older contemporary, Ibn Tofail,[38] held that whatever is produced must have an efficient cause. Similar views can be found among all the Jewish philosopher-theologians of the Middle Ages.

When we consider the views of the thirteenth-century Christian writers it is necessary to keep in mind that the several maxims of causality, causation, and the resemblance of causes and effects are not usually stated as separate principles. The reason for this is not far to seek. As inheritors of the Aristotelian and Neoplatonic doctrines, they conceived of causal connection in terms which do not permit any radical distinction of this kind. Thus in Grosseteste's statement we have these three principles together: "For if everything which is effected is effected by something similar to itself either specifically or proportionally, it is clear that the act of a potency precedes the potency either according to species or according to

34. Ibid.
35. *The Philosophy and Theology of Averroes*, trans. Mohammed Jamil-Ur-Rehman (Barolda, 1921), pp. 220 ff.; cf. p. 277.
36. Van den Berg, trans., *Incoherence*, pp. 318-19; cf. p. 273.
37. M. Horton, *Die Hauptlehren Averoes nach seiner Widerlegung Gazalis* (Bonn, 1913), p. 296.
38. *Hayy ibn Yagdhan, roman philosophique d'Ibn Thofail*, trans. Leon Gauthier (Beirut, 1936), sec. 49.

proportion."[39] The number and variety of formulations of the maxims of Aquinas are bewilderingly many. Nothing comes from potency to act, save by a being already in act.[40] Whatever does not exist, begins to be only by something which exists.[41] Whatever did not always exist, obviously has a cause.[42] The term cause, according to Aquinas, involves some influx into the caused being.[43] Moreover, everything which exists must either cause or be caused.[44]

The uniform action of causes, excepting miraculous events and the action of free agents, is set forth as a basic principle.[45] And a genuine plurality of causes for a given kind of effect is excluded.[46] These principles are explicitly called necessary.[47]

The most acute criticisms of causal maxims in the Middle Ages were developed in the fourteenth century probably as a result of the condemnation of "Averroism" in 1277. Many indications occur before William Ockham, for example, in the remarks of Henry of Harclay and Petrus Aureoli. Ockham stated that it is impossible to have unqualified certainty that finite or secondary causes are efficacious, because it could always be maintained that God is the cause of every effect ascribed to a secondary cause.[48] The medieval view that God can do anything without cooperating with natural causes that He can do by cooperating with them lies at the basis of this contention. Moreover, the only method of detecting causes which Ockham allows is this: if a change occurs in the presence and proximity of a given object and if it did not occur prior to this presence and proximity and if all other conditions are constant, then the object may

39. *De Potentia et Actu*, vol. 9 of *Beiträge zur Geschichte der Philosophia des Mittelalters* (Münster, 1912), p. 129.

40. *Summa Theologiae*, I, q. 2, a. 3; *Summa contra Gentiles*, I, 16.

41. *Summa Theologiae*, I, q. 2, a. 3.

42. *Summa Theologiae*, I, q. 46, a. 1.

43. In 5 *Meta.*, lect. I, *De Potentia et Actu* (*Beiträge zur Geschichte der Philosophia des Mittelalters*; Münster, 1908).

44. *Summa contra Gentiles*, iii, 107.

45. *De Generatione et Corruptione*, II, 10; *Physics*, IV, 14; *Compendium Theologiae*, I, 96.

46. *De Caelo et Mundo Expositio*, II, 24.

47. *Metaphysicorum Expositio*, IX, 4, n. 1818; *De Potentia et Actu*, III, 13; *Summa Theologiae*, I-II, q. 75, a. 1.

48. *Sentences*, 2, 9.5.

be regarded as the cause of the change. While Ockham himself never doubted the maxims of causality and causation and the like, his younger contemporaries who came under the influence of his writings certainly did.

The most thorough criticism with which we are acquainted at present was undertaken by Nicolas of Autrecourt.[49] From those of his writings which survive we find the following main contentions:

(1) It is not possible to infer, with the kind of evidence that depends on the principle of contradiction, the existence or non-existence of one thing from that of another.

(2) It is impossible to discover from observation and with certainty that any object or event causes any other object or event.

(3) The arguments which have been used to establish such maxims as *ex nihilo nihil* are purely verbal. Though certain conclusions may follow logically from describing changes or objects in certain ways, neither logic nor experience provides any reason for so describing such objects or changes.

The merely verbal force of the arguments to prove the existence of a substratum was clearly seen by Nicolas. In one of his letters he stated that if "natural transmutation is the acquisition of something in a subject with the destruction of a previous thing in the same subject, I concede that the following inference is valid: There is natural transmutation, therefore there is a subject." However, it is neither evident in itself nor by experience that there is any such transmutation. Likewise, if we understand that *accident* signifies something in a subject, we can argue that *there is an accident, therefore there is a substance*. Now some argue that, because whiteness is an accident, we can infer that whenever whiteness is perceived we can infer the existence of a substance. But Nicolas points out that neither by experience nor in itself is it evident that whatever is an accident. If such arguments were allowed, "anything whatever could be validly proved. For if it is laid down that the word *man* signified *A man is with a donkey*, it is obvious that from *A man exists* it follows that *A donkey exists*."

49. See *Epistola Magistri Nicholai de Autricort ad Bernardum*, ed. J. Lappe, vol. 6, pt. 2, in *Beiträge zur Geschichte der Philosophie der Mittelalters* (Münster, 1908), pp. 6-14; J. R. Weinberg, *Nicholas of Autrecourt* (Princeton, 1948; Greenwood Press, 1969).

Likewise, "if by *natural agents* you mean *those agents which are brought near their patients and without impediments bring about their action*, then it certainly follows that if a natural agent is brought near a patient and there is no impediment, action occurs. But I say that it is not evident by the kind of evidence in question either that such agents exist in the universe or that they may be posited. For if all things required for an effect are set forth I can hold without any contradiction which could be used against me that the effect will not occur." I believe that such arguments can be fairly compared with what Hume had to say about the argument that because every effect has a cause, every event has a cause.

Autrecourt's arguments, or arguments very like them, can be found in a number of Scholastics among his contemporaries and successors into the early fifteenth century. Moreover, the main propositions condemned against Nicolas are printed in fifteenth-century editions of Peter Lombard's *Sentences*[50] (1488). One of the authors who repeats some of his sceptical views is Pierre d'Ailly, who is quoted by Malebranche. This may suggest that there was some connection, however, indirect, between Nicolas, who was called by Dean Rashdall the "medieval Hume," and David Hume himself. But in my opinion such a suggestion is mistaken. It is very probable that Malebranche got his reference from a very careless reading of Suarez.[51]

Although historical influence seems to me improbable in the extreme, it is still worth asking to what extent Nicolas anticipated Hume's critique of causality and causation. Now it is beyond doubt, I believe, that the negative arguments are all to be found in Nicolas' surviving writings. There may even have been a hint of Hume's positive theory of causal belief in one statement of Nicolas.

It was a doctrine of Scotus that we can know such universals as *Rhubarb cures biliousness* or *Magnets attract iron* by adding to the data of induction the self-evident proposition that whatever results in many cases from a natural (that is, an unfree) cause, is its natural effect. Nicolas' reply to this is as follows: "Concerning things known by experience in the manner in which 'Rhubarb cures biliousness,' or 'A magnet attracts iron', we have only a *habitus conjecturativus* but

---

50. A treatise originally composed around 1150, in four volumes.
51. *Disputationes Metaphysicae*, XVIII.

not certitude. When it is asserted that we have certitude about such things by virtue of this proposition vesting in the soul, 'whatever happens in many cases from a natural cause is its natural effect', I put this question: What do you call *natural cause*; do you say that which, produced in the past and up to the present will do so in the future if it remains and is again applied? If so, I say that it is not known that what has then behaved in the past and present need do so in the future." It is barely possible that the phrase *habitus conjecturativus* means "habit productive of conjecture." It is more likely that it means only the possession of skill in conjecturing. If it means the former, of course, we have a suggestion of Hume's theory.

Nicolas did not develop Hume's psychological theory of causal belief, and neither Nicolas nor any other Scholastic attempted to account for the universal belief that causal connections are necessary. Despite Nicolas's scepticism about the possibility of knowledge of causes, he seems to continue to think of causal connection as objectively necessary. Hume, as we all know, holds that we have no idea of cause, objectively considered, other than constant conjunction. Although Nicolas disallows any experimental knowledge of causal connection, he continues to believe that experience of power and resistance affords some probability of the existence of causes and power. So far then as concerns the originality of Hume, the crucial point that we cannot attach any meaning to objective causal connection other than constant conjunction is not to be found among medieval writers.

This is not to say that the basic principles of the association of ideas were Hume's own discoveries. Some observations on the effects of association were made by Aristotle in *On Memory and Reminiscence*,[52] and the origin of the apothegm that habit is second nature goes back to Aristotle.[53] Avicenna[54] applied the principles of mnemonic association to the habitual expectation manifested by animals. Leibniz[55] held that such expectations are an imitation of

52. 449^b-453^b.

53. *Nicomachean Ethics*, vii, 9, 1152^a31.

54. *Kitab al-Najat*, trans. as *Avicenna's Psychology* by F. Rahman (London: Oxford University Press, 1952), Bk. III, ch. 6, p. 81.

55. *Monadology*, sec. 26; *New Essays Concerning Human Understanding*, trans. A. G. Langley (La Salle, Ill.: Open Court, 1949), II, ch. 11, sect. 11 (pp. 145-47).

reasoning, characteristic of animals and mere empirics. Hobbes, Spinoza, Locke, and Berkeley also had something to say about association. It was Hume's contribution to unite a theory of causal belief based on association with the negative critique of causation. This was, perhaps, the principal novelty of Hume's philosophy so far as the subject of cause is concerned.

It is necessary, for completeness, to add that several philosophical writers of the seventeenth century anticipated a part of Hume's criticism of the alleged discernment of causal efficacy. It has been pointed out by a number of scholars that these anticipations occur among the Occasionalists, and Hume's special indebtedness to Malebranche has been observed by most of the recent students of Hume's philosophy. Joseph Glanville's *Vanity of Dogmatizing* (1661) also contains a similar anticipation. Dugald Stewart (1792–1818) found an interesting observation in Barrow's *Mathematical Lectures*, in which it is stated that necessary consequence is to be found only in mathematics, so that "there can be no such connection of an external efficient cause with its effect (at least none such can be understood by us) . . . ."[56]

Hume could have had access to the ancient sceptics through Cicero's writings and from Fabricius' Latin edition of Sextus Empiricus (1718) or the French translation of 1725. He could have read accounts of Medieval occasionalism in the many available editions of Aquinas' *Contra Gentiles*, and his curiosity might have led him to investigate those schoolmen who denied the efficacy of second causes mentioned by Malebranche and Berkeley. But aside from the influences of the ancient sceptics and of Malebranche, which are undeniable, we shall probably never know how many of the anticipations of his critique were known to him. Nor is this very important. For Hume's special innovation was to have added a positive theory of causal belief to his failure to find necessary connection in the world accessible to the senses. No previous student of the subject had gone so far. But how consistently did Hume adhere to this discovery?

Sometimes he speaks as though there is a system of causes forever closed to us and distinct from causes in the meaning of that term of

56. Dugald Stewart, *Philosophy of the Human Mind* (London, 1856), pp. 552–54.

which we can make any sense. If he was serious in this, his views are plainly incoherent, and it is very difficult, without special pleading, to exonerate him from the charge of inconsistency or at least inexcusable looseness in these passages. It was the style of writers of his time to engage in declamations on the limits of our knowledge, and Hume fell in with this tendency. But the insight which influenced many writers on causal connection after him can, nevertheless, be cited as one of his principal contributions to modern thought.

HUME'S CONTRIBUTION TO INDUCTION

I turn now to Hume's contribution to induction. After having removed the grounds for holding that causality is logically certifiable, Hume pointed out that causation or the principle of uniformity is in a like position. It is neither intuitively nor demonstratively certain that as things have been so they will be. Hume then went on to argue, successfully, I believe, that this principle cannot be rendered probable by any appeal to experience. Although this point has often been disputed, the issues are so well know that it is not necessary to resume them here.   The previous history of attempts to rationalize induction will bring out how radical Hume's innovation was.

Aristotle appealed to *nous* as the faculty by which we form universal concepts from repetition of observation and by which the basic principles of arts and sciences are ascertained. The Epicureans also put much stock in the confirmations of our initial conviction by subsequent observation, and even the Stoics somewhat grudgingly assign a place to inductive reasoning. Only the ancient sceptics of the Pyrrhonic persuasion raised doubt about induction.

In Sextus Empiricus[57] the inductive syllogism is criticized on the ground that we cannot be sure that we have surveyed all the species of a genus. Elsewhere, Sextus holds that the induction from individual to species may be criticized on the grounds that if only some of the particulars are examined, the induction can be refuted by a yet undiscovered counter-instance, and that, since it is impossible to review all of the individuals whose number is either infinite or

57. *Purrhōneior Hupotupōseis*, II, 195.

indefinite, induction cannot be secured.[58] The suggestion later made
by Hume that appeals to experience in this matter are question-
begging does not seem to have occurred to the ancient sceptics,
although they maintained that some deductive inferences beg the
question.

The important medieval speculations about the rationale of
induction begin with Avicenna, whose views on this subject seem to
have been communicated to the Christian scholastics by way of
Al-Ghazali's paraphrase of Avicenna's *Logic*. According to Avicenna,
induction by simple enumeration is, as Francis Bacon later observed,
subject to refutation by a single counter-instance.[59] It is always
possible that the unobserved instances differ from the observed
instances no matter how numerous the latter may be. This criticism
is essentially the same as that found in Sextus Empiricus. But, despite this, Avicenna held that observation, when supplemented by
some general principle, can yield universal knowledge. In several
places he repeats essentially the same argument: If we sensibly observe a concomitance in past observation, the mind unconsciously
produces a syllogism whose major premise is that what happens very
frequently cannot be due to chance or coincidence. This premise was
derived from Aristotle.[60] From this unconscious syllogism, the general conclusion is drawn that events will always be thus in the future.
This argument was used by later Muslim and Jewish philosophers in
the Middle Ages. Pines has found it in Abu-I-Barakat, and it occurs
again in Mordecai Cominto's commentary on a logical work of
Maimonides. It is essentially this argument, with some additions,
which can be found in Grosseteste's commentary on Aristotle's
Posterior Analytics i, 14 and in Albertus Magnus.[61]

In the writings of Duns Scotus[62] we find a somewhat different
rationale of the passage from particular observations to the universal
proposition. The same is true of Ockham.[63] Both of them, however,

58. Ibid., 204 ff.
59. Avicenna, *Danesh-nameh*, trans. Achenna and Masse, I, 61; Francis
Bacon, *Novum Organum*, Bk. II, 105.
60. *Physics*, ii, 4, 196^{b}10-13.
61. *Analytica Posteriora*, i, tract 1, ch. 2.
62. *Opus Oxoniense*, i, d. 3, q. 4, in R. McKeon, *Selections from Medieval
Philosophers* (New York: Scribners, 1929), vol. 2, p. 329.
63. *Quodlibet Septem*, v, q. 2, in McKeon, vol. 2, pp. 375-80.

require that observation be supplemented by some general proposition which recommends itself to our reason in order to obtain universal causal propositions. There is certainly much indirect evidence from the writings of Bacon, Galileo, and others that such general propositions were appealed to. Leibniz is quite explicit about this. In his "Preface to an edition of Nizolius,"[64] he holds that the universal propositions to be added to the data of induction must not themselves depend on induction but must depend on "a universal idea or definition of terms." One of these propositions is that *If the cause is the same or similar, the effect will be the same or similar.* Leibniz states that if such propositions were themselves based on induction, we should be involved in an infinite regress. But none of these authors, so far as I have observed, was aware that the universal propositions which would suffice to make an induction certain or probable could not be logically certified. With the exception of Leibniz, none saw clearly that an appeal to experience to establish any principle of inductive inference leads to an infinite regress.

The clear realization of these points can be fairly accredited to Hume. It is true that Autrecourt saw the verbal character of Scotus' principle of induction. But no one before Hume pointed out that, because every appeal to experience presupposes that unexamined cases resemble the examined cases of the generalization to be established, any such appeal to experience to establish the resemblance of the unexamined and the examined cases would beg the question.

The importance of this discovery of Hume has been obscured. Some philosophers have supposed that Hume denied that we would ever find that a given future resembles a given past. Hume's actual point was the quite different one, namely, that we can never discover *beforehand* that our expectations of such a resemblance are going to be fulfilled.

THE MERITS OF HUME'S EXPLANATION
OF NECESSARY CONNECTION

There has been altogether too much argument in the history of philosophy. The practice of elucidating philosophical difficulties by

---

64. *Die Philosophischen Schriften von G. F. Leibniz*, ed. C. J. Gerhardt, 7 vols. (Berlin, 1875-90), IV, 138-76; Leroy Loemker, *Leibniz: Philosophical Papers and Letters*, 2 vols. (Chicago, 1956), I, 201.

the study of the ways in which people fall into linguistic traps has been very popular among us in recent times. It has undoubted value, and it is perhaps true that it is sometimes the only method that serves to dispel the bewilderment over some philosophical confusions. Yet this method has some bad features. It is altogether too easy to avoid the responsibilities of argument by assuming that an intellectual opponent had better be treated as the unfortunate victim of a philosophical disease. Hume's method with the prevalent views about necessary causal connection is an admirable *media via*.

It was only after Hume had extensively examined the arguments of his contemporaries and predecessors which purported to establish the principles of causality, causation, and the like as necessary truths, and only after an elaborate investigation of the various effects of belief, that he at length proposed his own theory about the origin of the idea of necessity. This theory involves the exposure of a confusion and, in Hume's view, a resulting misuse of the term *cause*. The technique itself was not new. Examples of this technique can be found throughout the history of Western philosophy. To consider one instance, among many, Ockham's elucidations of the concepts of place, time, and motion all begin by attempts to refute views Ockham considered mistaken. Eventually, Ockham attempts to locate the source of the views he considered erroneous in some misunderstanding of the functions of discourse. What was novel in Hume's case was the application of the technique to the particular case of *necessary connection* and the definition of cause.

There is a presumption which must be made in philosophical criticism similar to the one which should be made at the outset of a legislative debate, namely, that one's opponent is not a fool. This means that exposure of error or confusion should precede psychological diagnosis of the sources of errors or confusions. To do less than this violates the minimum conditions of intellectual exchange. That Hume in general followed this principle constitutes one mark of superiority over some of his latter-day followers.

It is worth noticing that Hume retains the four main propositions which, since Aristotle, had been generally maintained about causal connection, namely, that every beginning or new modification of anything has a cause, that similar causes have similar effects and that similar effects have similar causes, and finally, that a cause must be adequate to its effect.[65] Hume never tired of informing his readers that, considered *a priori,* anything can cause anything. So it is entirely clear that for Hume none of these propositions is logically certifiable. MacNabb has found evidence that Hume believed that the principle that whatever begins has a cause is based on scientific experience, and it is plausible to suppose that Hume denied the plurality of causes and affirmed the need of an adequate cause of a given effect because he thought that our experience would support such beliefs. It is, of course, far from clear that this is the case. In any case the opportunity for investigating the consequences of a genuine plurality of causes was passed over.

HUME'S NOMINALISM

However essential to his main philosophical views or to his own way of stating those views the nominalism of Hume may have been, Hume did not introduce any essentially new ideas of very far-reaching importance under this head. It is possible that, in one way or another, the critique of abstraction undertaken by the medieval nominalists had some influence on Berkeley and Hume. But whether or not there was any influence, the central tenets of nominalism had already been elaborated in the fourteenth century, and the views of Berkeley and Hume add nothing to the negative or critical aspect of the question. Moreover, the medieval statement of the nominalist position is, in important ways, superior to what Berkeley and Hume have to say on the subject. A central tenet of Hume's nominalism is that whatever is distinguishable is separable. As far as I have been able to discover, Hume never supports this by any argument or evidence, and it is therefore a sheer dogma in his philosophy. On the other hand, the most effective representative of medieval nominalism, Ockham, has an elaborate argument to support this proposition.

It is only in his positive theory that Hume has something new to say, namely his explanation of how, despite the numerical singularity and radically determinate nature of an idea, it may represent individuals which differ from one another either numerically or

65. *Enquiry Concerning Human Understanding,* sec. xi; *Dialogues Concerning Natural Religion,* Dialogue iv, pp. 160-61 of Kemp-Smith edition; *Treatise of Human Nature,* I, 3, 15.

specifically. This is the doctrine that other ideas are associated with the representative idea and can be recalled by necessity or design.

The real importance of Hume's nominalism appears in his radical suggestions with regard to bodies and minds. The novelty of this part of Hume's thought remains to be dealt with. Before doing so, I must discuss his negative critique of physical and mental substance.

Some of Hume's criticisms of the conception of substance and of our alleged knowledge of substance could have been derived from certain ancient and medieval philosophers. In fact, Hume has remarkably little to say on this question. He held, firstly, that we can assign no meaning to the term *substance* if we intend by it something specifically different from our perceptions,[66] or as he put it earlier, "we have no idea of substance, distinct from that of a collection of particular qualities."[67] Now, in addition to what he doubtless learned from Berkeley's critique of material substances in the *Principles of Human Knowledge* and Locke's diffidence on the subject in the *Essay*, there were probably other sources which were accessible to him which raised questions on this head. There were many other writers who had similar doubts, especially among the later medieval writers. To cite a few, we consider first Francis de Marchia, who in about 1320 in Paris wrote that "our mind, in the present life, does not have any proper concept of substance, neither essential nor quidditative . . . but only has a proper negative concept and a proper positive accidental concept. . . . The reason for this is that substance, in this life, does not through itself and immediately move our intellect but only by means of an accident, because substance only moves the intellect by means of sensation which is not capable of [apprehending] substance."[68] Ockham wrote to much the same effect in his *Questions on the Sentences*,[69] and Nicolas of Autrecourt held that the language of "inherence" was plainly derived from observation, and that it was an external analogy used to characterize something with which we can have no direct acquaintance. That we can have no proper concept of the material subject of change goes

66. *Treatise of Human Nature*, I, 4, 2.
67. Ibid., I, 1, 6.
68. *Sent.* I, d. 3, q. 31. (Leipzig) U. B. Cod. ms 352 fol 46. Translated from the quotation given in Erich Hochstetter, "Nominalismus?" *Franciscan Studies*, 9 (1949), 384.
69. *Sentences*, I, d. 3, q. 10.

back to the Democritean distinction between what we know by convention and what exists in truth. That the receptacle of change can only be known by a bastard reasoning is explicitly stated in Plato's *Timaeus.* Aristotle held that prime matter can be known only "according to an analogy." Thus, although the immediate source of Hume's views was undoubtedly Berkeley's critique of materialism, the difficulties were noticed again and again in ancient and medieval thought.

The germs of the critique of our *knowledge* of material substance go back to ancient scepticism. The sceptical critique of the Stoic cataleptic phantasy and the distinction between admonitive and indicative signs contain the principles by which Hume's "scepticism with regard to the senses" could have been developed. The question is whether anything in our experience is an unerring sign of transempirical reality. The arguments of Carneades and the later sceptics could have provided some of the basis for Hume's critique.

In the fourteenth century, a number of philosophers rejected the idea that we know matter or nature directly or intuitively, and suggested that inference is surely involved, although some, for example Walter Burley, suggested that the inference is an unconscious one (Albert of Saxony, Walter Burleigh, et al.).

A number of writers suggested that no inference of this kind can be demonstrative (Fitz-Ralph, Marsilius of Inghen), for reasons very like those offered by Hume. Marsilius and others, however, held that probable arguments could be given for the existence of substances. Nicolas of Autrecourt, however, went further and anticipated Hume's argument in the *Treatise* and the *Enquiry*[70] that arguments from experience cannot establish the existence of any substance. According to Nicolas, a person has probable knowledge of one thing, given the existence of another, only if at some time it was evident that the two occurred together. But since past experience reveals no conjunction between appearances and their allegedly substantial basis, there can be no probable knowledge of substances.

In the history of Western philosophy before the eighteenth century, I have found no evidence either conclusive or even presumptive that doubts about the existence of the self were raised similar to those for which Hume was noted.

70. *Treatise,* I, 4, 7; *Enquiry,* sec. 12, pt. 1.

Before Hume, there were two main lines of discussion about the knowledge of the self. The philosophers of predominantly Neoplatonic or Augustinain persuasion tended to claim that the self is known directly. Those who followed Aristotle more closely favored the doctrine that the self is known indirectly by way of a knowledge of the acts of the soul. If we go back to Plato we find in the *First Alcibiades*, 133, the suggestion that self-knowledge consists in the self contemplating its highest—the knowing—part. Since this dialogue was used as a sort of textbook by the Neoplatonists, it is probable that Plotinus derived his views from this source. It is suggested by Aristotle, too, in the *De Anima*,[71] that there is identity of knowledge and the known in beings devoid of matter. Elsewhere, however, while Aristotle holds the view that there is a sensation of sensation,[72] he seems to hold that the knowledge of the essence of the soul can only be obtained by first studying its operations and powers. Some of the commentators, such as Alexander and Themistius, hold that we are aware that we are aware. The most emphatic statement of this self-awareness and of its being a function of the rational soul was that of Philoponus.[73]

The emphasis on direct self-knowledge of the soul by itself is to be found in Plotinus,[74] from which, probably, Augustine derived the notion. In his work *De Trinitate*[75] Augustine insists that the mind knows itself by means of itself. Many of the Franciscans followed Augustine in this doctrine. We should cite Bonaventure[76] and Matthew of Aquasparta as examples. Aquinas, on the other hand, contended that the mind knows itself only by way of knowing its acts.[77]

The doctrine of direct self-knowledge is a distinctive feature of Avicenna's philosophy and is used by him for several diverse purposes.

71. iii, 4, 432^{a}2.

72. *Nicomachean Ethics*, i, 9, 1170^{a}29 ff.; *De Somno*, 2, 455^{a}16.

73. *On De Anima*, iii, 2, 425^{b}12.

74. *The Enneads*, v. 9, 4.

75. ix, 3.3.

76. *Commentary on the Sentences*, II, 39, 1, 2, Conclusion; *De Mysterio Trinitatis*, I, 1, 10.

77. *Summa Theologiae*, Part I, q. 87, a. 1.

Some indications of scepticism about self-knowledge are suggested in some fourteenth-century writers. Then Ockham, while he holds that the inner states of consciousness are as evident as, or perhaps more evident than, knowledge of outer objects, denies that we can have any demonstration that the soul is immortal. In general, however, as critical of absolute certainty about external objects as some fourteenth-century Scholastics were, there is little evidence of any application of this criticism to the knowledge of self, mind, or soul. We find several anticipations of the argument for which Descartes is famous throughout the Middle Ages from the time of Augustine.

Neither Locke nor Leibniz had doubts about the existence of the self, but it is probably Locke who gave Hume some suggestion that personal identity may be a far more complicated affair than had been hitherto supposed. His suggestion that matter may have the capacity to think, and the further suggestion that the continuity of the self depends on mnemonic experience rather than the direct inspection of the essence of the soul by itself, must have contributed something to Hume's views. But this was all.

It is, therefore, not too much to say that Hume's doubts about a single identical substance persisting numerically unchanged throughout psychic life was largely his own. His view of causal connection rendered useless the arguments that material things cannot produce psychical events. His insistence that some perceptions are spatially located while others are incapable of spatial location was, for him, conclusive evidence that the "question concerning the substance of the soul" was unintelligible. To this must be added that Hume could attach no clear notion to the terms *substance* and *inherence,* whether material or psychical substances are in question.

Hume's positive theories about the nature of body and mind are also largely his own. No doubt Locke's doctrines about nominal essences and Berkeley's construction of material things as collections of qualities contributed, but the theories of personal identity and of our belief in bodies were quite original, and paved the way for phenomenalism and positivism.

There is an unfortunate tendency today to downgrade Hume's psychological theories concerning the origin of belief in bodies and in the self. The deficiencies of these theories, Hume's own dissatisfaction, and the advances in philosophy in the past thirty-five years account for this in large measure. The correct evaluation of Hume's contribution to these subjects must, however, be made in terms of what went before. Thus considered, the complexities of physical and psychical things require that they be seen as processes or as systems, as Hume called them. Hume's account of the nature of bodies and selves may have been nothing less than the intellectual disaster that David Pears intimates it was. Nevertheless, the complexities of our cognition of bodies and selves, which Hume emphasized more strongly than any of his predecessors, made it forever impossible to return to earlier views of these subjects. For such views depended on a doctrine of substance which even long before Hume had been subject to serious criticism. Hume's negative criticisms and his constructive theories both, but for different reasons, contributed to the eventual abandonment of the notion. And it is fair to say that Hume's original contributions here, even if they ultimately proved to be untenable, brought to light complexities in the problem which were not realized or understood by earlier philosophers.

There are important parts of Hume's philosophy which are now obsolete. It is not an act of daring to declare that these parts have been definitely refuted. In particular, that part of his scepticism which depends on the assumptions of the privacy of the realm of impressions and ideas to which each person has privileged access has collapsed under the scrutiny it has received in the last thirty-five years. Nominalism, as Hume presented it at least, is not, I think, capable of resurrection. In fact, his theories of thinking, of the nature of abstraction, and many other related matters must be put away into the mausoleum of intellectual history. Yet even here, his speculations, in the perspective of history, may have performed an important service. Though his positive and constructive theories on all these questions have proved to be mistaken, his work showed that we cannot answer the questions and solve the problems in ways philosophers before him had used. His novelties, both the successes and the failures, advanced most of the important fields of philosophical inquiry beyond the state in which he found them. And this, perhaps, is as much as we have a right to expect of any contributor to such a perennially problematic subject as philosophy is and ought only to be.

10

Two Recent
Criticisms of Hume

In 1962 G. E. M. Anscombe offered some criticisms of Hume's argument in *Treatise of Human Nature*, Book I, Part 3, Section 3, where he attempted to show that the causal maxim *whatever has a beginning must have a cause* is neither intuitive nor demonstratively certain. According to Miss Anscombe,

> Either he [sc. Hume] is confusing the two propositions:
> (i) 'Necessarily, if anything begins to exist, something causes it' and (ii) 'If anything begins to exist, then of something it holds necessarily that it causes that thing' . . . But it is only to (ii) that Hume's arguments apply with any force . . . *or*, if Hume was genuinely discussing (i) rather than (ii), he relied on an argument from imagination to assure us that "Something has come into existence without any cause' describes a possible state of affairs. But imagination can have no authority here. All it can do is to supply us with as it were a picture of something coming into existence, without a picture of a cause annexed, the title under the picture being "picture of something coming into existence without any cause."[1]

1. G. E. M. Anscombe, "Hume Reconsidered," *Blackfriars*, 43 (1962), p. 188.

As this accusation of fallacious reasoning has been repeated in a somewhat garbled form by Anthony Kenny in 1962[2] without any disapproval and with explicit acknowledgment to Miss Anscombe, it would seem worthwhile to show first where it fails.

The second criticism is easiest to deal with first. As it was put, it contains an obvious error. If it really had been Hume's intention merely to hold that the imagination can present us with a beginning without annexing a picture of its being caused, the picture Miss Anscombe wrote about was surely misdescribed. It should have been "Picture of something beginning," and not "Picture of something beginning without a cause." For if the picture is given the latter title, it establishes that Hume was not guilty of the fallacy in question. In order to show this, we must reexamine Hume's original statement in the light of the historical background.

Hume, as we all know, rejected the classical theories of abstraction which had been expressed, in various forms, since the time of Aristotle.[3] The medievals, as well as Descartes, recognized two distinct operations of the mind: (1) abstraction, and (2) precision, or exclusion, or separation. The latter requires that (a) both objects that are distinguished be before the mind at the same time, and (b) we discern, at that time, that one can exist and the other not exist without any ensuing contradiction. Descartes makes this point out in great detail in the *Replies to Objections* and in letters to Arnauld, Gibieuf, and Mesland.[4]

If we assume, as I believe we may, that Hume knew very well the difference between *abstracting* and *distinguishing*, we may assume that his point was not that I can think of *beginning* without thinking of *being caused* but rather than I can think of *beginning without being caused*. A reexamination of the passage will bear this out. It runs thus:

2. Anthony Kenny, *The Five Ways* (New York: Shocken Books, 1969), p. 67.

3. Aristotle does not use *aphairesis* to describe all forms of the alleged activity of abstraction; in the genesis of mathematical concepts he speaks of abstraction, in other cases he uses other terms. The medievals, however, use *abstraction* simply. This probably goes back to Alexander of Aphrodisias.

4. Descartes to Gibieuf, 19 January 1642; Descartes to Mesland, Leyden, 2 May 1644 (?).

... as all distinct ideas are separable from each other, and as the ideas of cause and effect are evidently distinct, t'will be easy for us to conceive any object non-existent this moment and existent the next without conforming to it the distinct idea of a cause or productive principle. The separation, therefore, of the idea of a cause from that of a beginning of existence is plainly possible for the imagination; and consequently the actual separation of these objects is so far possible, that it implies no contradiction nor absurdity; and is therefore incapable of being refuted by any reasoning from mere ideas, without which it is impossible to demonstrate the necessity of a cause.[5]

Now if we neglected to notice that Hume is writing about ideas that have been distinguished, we might carelessly read this passage as meaning simply that because we can think of *A* without thinking of *B*, it follows that *A* can exist without *B*. This careless but plausible reading might have been further encouraged by the use of *conjoining.* For Hume often contrasts *conjoined* with *connected,*[6] But *conjunction, conjoin,* etc., have also a use which would justify another employment of these words. This can be verified by the historical notes in the Oxford English Dictionary and in the fact that the latin of *liaison necessaire* in Descartes' *Regulae* is sometimes *conjunctio necessaria* and occasionally *connexio necessaria.*[7] (The *Regulae* were published in 1701 and again in 1704.) But we need not go so far afield to make the point, for whatever *conjoining* meant, Hume's point surely was that we are not logically coerced into putting together two ideas which we have already discerned as distinct. It was certainly not the argument that the ability to think of one of them without thinking of the other proved the possibility of one of these objects existing without the other. But even if Hume meant what Miss Anscombe attributed to him, he would still have a case. For as he rejected the classical doctrine of abstraction, partially on the ground that we cannot think of one of two necessarily connected

5. David Hume, *Treatise of Human Nature*, I, 3, 3, Selby-Bigge ed., pp. 78 ff.
6. David Hume, *Enquiry Concerning Human Understanding*, Selby-Bigge ed., p. 70, par. 54, and p. 74, par. 58.
7. See esp. Regula XII, *AT*, x, pp. 420-21.

ideas clearly and distinctly without thinking of the other, the ability to think of one without thinking of the other would, in any case, depend on the ability to think one without the other. No doubt this is a bad argument. But it is not the crude mistake Miss Anscombe supposed it to be. In any case, I doubt that Hume was guilty of it. In seventeenth- and eighteenth-century philosophy, what the imagination can do is limited to what is logically possible, not the converse. Logical possibility was thought to determine psychological conceivability, not the other way around.

The other charge of fallacy was that Hume might have confused two propositions which would be rendered as follows: (1) necessary (y)[beginning $y \supset (\exists x)x$ causes y] ; (2) (y)[beginning $y \supset (\exists x)$ necessary, x causes y]. Now I think it very unlikely that Hume was guilty of this confusion, and I am equally disinclined to think that his arguments are effective only against the second.

For if Hume thought that in refuting the alleged necessity in the second proposition he also refuted the alleged necessity in the first, why in the world did he distinguish between the two propositions in the first place? The closest he comes, of course, to raising questions about the second is in asking "why such particular causes have such particular effects." These questions are dealt with in *Treatise of Human Nature*, I, 3, 6, and elsewhere in *Enquiry Concerning Human Understanding*. There is nothing in the nature of one object which indicates what sort of effect, if any, it will have. The characteristic features of any alleged cause provide no clue as to the feature of any effect it may have. And these arguments would apply with equal force if we were to attempt to surmise the nature of the cause of any alleged effect. The points to be made in both cases apply to the natures of causes and effects. And the fact that Hume separated the two sorts of questions is sufficient evidence that he did not confuse them.

It is true, of course, that the Scholastic and Cartesian views did not separate these questions. Both the Scholastics and Descartes supposed that the similarity of causes and effects, as well as the necessity of a cause for every event, depended on one proposition, viz., *ex nihilo nihil fit*. For the full meaning of the proposition that nothing comes from nothing was not only that the existence of an event required a cause, but also that the nature of such an event required a similar nature in its cause. Potentialities are necessarily actualized by some actual cause or other, but also by an actuality that is overtly or eminently like the actualized result. For reasons plain to anyone who follows Hume's strategy, he would not have been moved by the doctrines which had led others to run these considerations together.

In Mr. Anthony Kenny's version of this criticism (which he accredits to Miss Anscombe), both of the fallacies are committed. He does not argue for either charge, but is content to repeat what is in Miss Anscombe's article. In quoting the disputed passage, however, he omits the crucial beginning referring to the separability of distinct ideas, and so gives the misleading impression that Hume is simply arguing from *I can conceive of A without conceiving of B* to *I can conceive of A without B.* But, as I hope I have shown, the argument in Hume does not commit this simple-minded fallacy.

As both Miss Anscombe and Mr. Kenny express doubts not only about Hume's success in showing that the causal maxim is not a necessary truth but about whether anyone has shown this, it is perhaps worthwhile to reconsider the matter on its own merits apart from questions of Humian textual criticism.

Miss Anscombe also admits that the causal maxim can be denied without contradiction. But she thinks that the logically necessary extends beyond the class of propositions whose contradictions are self-contradictory. The example of a proposition whose contradictory is not self-contradictory but is a logically necessarily true proposition is *An expanse of color A and an expanse of color B cannot coincide if A and B are (determinately) different colors.* Now we have all been puzzled about how to understand or clarify such propositions, and the best results to date amount to treating color-predicates as definable predicates, and then construing *Nothing is both red and green all over* for example, as an analytic proposition. Still, as the matter is controversial and cannot be regarded as at all definitively settled, the example is a bad one.

But it is really beside the point, as far as the status of the causal maxim is concerned. The proposition was accepted because it was thought to be *per se nota,* and this was challenged by Al-Ghazali in the eleventh century and by Nicolas of Autrecourt (and many others) in the fourteenth century on the grounds that it was not *per se nota.*

What did this phrase *per se nota* mean to the medievals, or for that matter, to the seventeenth- and eighteenth-century philosophers? It certainly meant a proposition whose denial is logically absurd, in other words self-contradictory. Now we can freely admit that Hume had no very clear view of what this amounts to, but neither did his predecessors nor contemporaries. But we are in a better position. For in the propositional calculus and the lower predicate calculus we have available clear definitions of *contradictory* and *analytic*. (That we do not have a universally applicable definition of these terms does not affect the question of the status of the causal maxim, because it is concerned only with states of affairs which can be represented in the Lower Predicate Calculus with identity.)

Now the question really boils down to this: Does the minimal definition of *to begin* logically entail *to be caused*? Hume argued that it did not, on the ground that *to begin* simply means *to be after not having been*, and this obviously does not entail *to be caused*, whatever the latter phrase means. It is true that of any object or event x there are attributes true of x and known to be true of x other than the fact that x was not always around. But none of these additional known facts about x (short of there being some y that caused x) imply that there is a y that caused x. Of course, x can be described in terms of relational attributes which imply this. But then the question always comes up about the warrant for so describing x. All this, I am sure, is well known, but it deserved repetition when we are confronted with the criticisms I have been discussing.

The curious view persists that Hume's view about the nonlogical character of the causal maxim depends on peculiarities of his psychological theories, or his deficiencies as a logician, or again, his metaphysical dogma that distinguishables are always separable. As *he* presents his view, all these difficulties may be present. But his essential insight can be restated in a way that is free from them. Such a restatement will, of course, not be Hume. But modern philosophy is largely indebted to Hume for the discovery, as Kant has witnessed.

11

Kenny, Hume, and Causal Necessity

Anthony Kenny, following in the footsteps of G. E. M. Anscombe, declares that there are two fallacies in Hume's *Treatise of Human Nature* (I, 3, 3). The first is that Hume illegitimately infers from *conceiving B without conceiving C* to *conceiving B without C*. The second is the "fallacious shifting of modal operations." The second accusation is put in the format of a footnote as follows: "The fallacious move is from $\sim(y)(By\supset(\exists x)LPxy)$ to $\sim(y)L(By\supset(\exists x)Pxy)$.[1]

Now it is not at all obvious from Hume's text that either of these fallacies has been committed. This is not to say, of course, that the passage in Hume is a model of clarity; indeed, I do not see how any reconstruction of this passage could be guaranteed, because a number of different reconstructions could be made. But there are historical reasons for rejecting the first accusation of fallacy. As far as the second accusation of fallacy is concerned, I think I can show that Hume's doctrine can be more plausibly construed in another way which will clear him of the charge.

There are many discussions in Descartes which concern this very

---

1. Anthony Kenny, *The Five Ways* (New York: Shocken Books, 1969), p. 67. In the footnote, *Lp* means *Necessarily P; Pxy* means *x brings y into existence; Bx* means *x begins to exist.* Logical notation has been recast into that of *Principia.*

141

problem. Descartes believed that abstraction is possible but not very useful; in fact, he thought it usually quite harmful. But he did believe that distinction was both possible and maximally useful. Now he also clearly distinguished between a concept rendered inadequate by abstraction and a concept clearly and distinctly conceived as distinct from another concept. This, at any rate, establishes the well-publicized difference between the two cases.

The crucial phrases in Hume are the following: "As all distinct ideas are separable from each other, and as the ideas of cause and effect are evidently distinct, t'will be easy for us to conceive any object to be non-existent this moment and existent the next without conjoining to it the distinct idea of a cause or productive principle"; and, "The actual separation of these objects is so far possible, that it implies no contradiction or absurdity."[2]

Now when Hume uses *conjoin* here he may well have meant conjoin in the sense in which he uses the term in the expression *constant conjunction* and in other cases in which *conjunction* is contrasted with *connection* or *necessary connection*. But he could also have used *conjoin* in a manner similar to Descartes' *liaison necessaire*, the Latin of which is *conjunctio necessaria*.[3] But however he may have meant conjoin when he was discussing distinct ideas, he may more plausibly be supposed to have had both of the ideas distinguished from one another before his mind, and have been attempting to say that we perceive nothing which obliges us to conjoin such two ideas in any sense of *conjoin*. As this interpretation is at least as plausible as the one suggested by Kenny, it at once releases Hume from the first charge of fallacy. For, on the interpretation I am proposing, Hume's meaning is simply that when we consider the very abstract ideas of *beginning* and *being caused*, we see no logically compelling reason that prevents us from affirming one of whatever it is true of, and denying the other of that same object.

The second charge is much more difficult to refute, because it is difficult to find in the relevant passage anything to which it could possibly apply. I do not see that Hume was under any necessity to make the alleged move from the premise to the conclusion, because,

2. Both passages occur in the *Treatise of Human Nature*, I, 3, 3, Selby-Bigge ed., pp. 78–79.

3. *Regulae*, XII, *AT*, x, pp. 420–21.

in a sense, he has already arrived at the conclusion via another route. I shall attempt to explain this. Hume claims that $(\exists y)(By \cdot \sim(\exists x)(Pxy))$ is not a contradiction. Of course, as I wrote before, Hume did not put it just this way because he did not have the notation of modern logic available. But by *necessity* in these passages, he clearly meant what we mean by *logical necessity*. And, if so, my formulation is closer to Hume's intentions than any use of modal operations where the modals are *de re* and not *de dicto*. I do not deny, of course, that some of his formulations lend themselves to a *de re* interpretation.[4] Some, however, lend themselves just as easily to the *de dicto* reading.[5]

The formulation I have given the conclusion of the argument from the distinction to the separation would bring us at once to recognize that *There are beginnings without causes* is logically possible, that is, free from contradiction. In fact, if the first charge is dropped, I do not see how the second could be made.

On my interpretation of the disputed passage, the necessity of a cause for every beginning of existence makes *necessity* apply to the whole proposition. Thus, if modals are involved, $L(y)[By \supset (\exists x)Pxy]$. But, since Hume is here concerned with that notion of necessity which was construed as that the denial of which involves contradiction, the modern notion of analyticity would be a propos. Thus, analytic $(y)[By \supset (\exists x)Pxy]$ so that contradictory $(\exists y)[By \cdot \sim(\exists x)Pxy]$. Now Hume's argument shows that $(\exists y)[By \cdot \sim(\exists x)Pxy]$ is not contradictory if B (= begins) is given its minimal meaning. For, it is only when we pack much more than *to be after not having been* into *beginning* that we have any chance of producing a contradictory proposition of $(\exists y)[By \cdot \sim(\exists x)Pxy]$. It will be noted that Hume does not have to be concerned with what *x producing y* means (although it has to mean something if we are to have a proposition at all). In fact, he does not tell us what *to produce* or *to cause* means until section 14 of the *Treatise of Human Nature*, I, 3. The whole issue rests on the meaning of *to begin*. There is nothing more to the matter.

The interpretation of modal operations is notoriously difficult, and, in any case, their application to Hume is questionable, to say the least. There is nothing in Hume's formulation of the principle

4. *Treatise*, I, 3, 3.
5. Ibid.

that every beginning has a cause which suggests that he meant anything like either of the formulae ascribed by Kenny and Anscombe.[6] Since Hume was concerned with notions which are equivalent to *analytic* and *contradictory*, and since these notions are defined for propositions and not for predicates, they would have application only in the way I have indicated.

6. G. E. M. Anscombe, "Hume Reconsidered," *Blackfriars*, 1962, p. 188.

III
CONTEMPORARY PHILOSOPHY

12

Relation
and Qualities

I want to discuss an argument which was presented in Lewis and Langford's *Symbolic Logic*[1] many years ago, and which seems to me a very powerful argument against Leibniz's view that relations are ideal or mental in the sense that the extradiscursive or extracognitive counterpart of relational expressions are qualitative states of individuals. As I have argued elsewhere and will not repeat here, the Leibnizian view has a long history going back to classical antiquity and is founded on the Aristotelian view that relations are accidents and that a given accident cannot belong to more than one individual.[2] So if the only extradiscursive or extramental realities are things and their accidents, relations as components of facts will be states of substances taken one at a time and not, as many philosophers since Russell have contended, features of facts which require (with some exceptions) two or more individuals taken together.

The argument in Lewis and Langford (which seems to have come from Langford)[3] is as follows.

1. C. I. Lewis and C. H. Langford, *Symbolic Logic* (New York: Century, 1932).
2. J. R. Weinberg, *Abstraction, Relation, and Induction* (Madison: University of Wisconsin Press, 1965), pp. 75–78.
3. *Symbolic Logic*, pp. 387 ff.

Consider the pair of formulae *(∃x)(y)xRy* and *(y)(∃x)Ry*. These two formulae, for all interpretations of *R*, mean plainly different things. The second follows logically from the first, but the converse inference is not valid. Now the proposal that these formulae can be replaced by formulae in which the dyadic relational expression can be replaced by a pair of monadic predicates can be shown to lead to inconvenient results. For assume that we replaced these formulae by others in the following way: for *(∃x)(y)xRy* put *(∃x)(y) Px·Qy* and for *(y)(∃x)xRy* put *(y)(∃)Px·Qy*.

It is easily seen that the replacements can also be expressed by *(∃x)Px·(y)Qy* and *(y)Qy·(∃x)Px*. Now since conjunction is commutative, this amounts to *(∃x)Px·(y)Qy* and *(∃x)Px·(y)Qy*. Thus we see that the replacements of two formulae with different meanings turn out to have exactly the same meaning, and this establishes that the proposal is unsuccessful, so that relational statements cannot be reduced to nonrelational statements.

It is necessary, however, to add to this argument several others, in order to make it entirely sure that the argument establishes what was almost certainly intended, viz., that a logical fact shows that a pre-Russellian interpretation of relational expressions is demonstrably false and that relations are a part of the ultimate furniture of the world—put another way, that relational expressions express not further reducible features of the extradiscursive world.

Faced with the aforementioned argument, a defender of the Aristotelico-Scholastic view of relations might retort that the formulation of the replacements was incorrect or incomplete. The correct or complete formulation should have been *(∃x)(y)Pⓨx·Qⓧy* and *(y)(∃x)Pⓨx·Qⓧy*, the significance of the circled *x* and *y* being this: a relational accident has the peculiarity that it is an accident of one thing which contains an inclination toward another thing or a reference to another thing. Now the natural way to express this reference or inclination would be to employ some symbolic device which would distinguish the referring expression contained in the accident, and accordingly I have chosen the circle. So the expression *Pⓨ* is to be understood as a single predicate expression standing for the relational accident in question.

Now it is quite easily shown that this does not, and cannot, accomplish the purpose intended. The intention was to prevent the move from *(∃x)(y)Pyx·Qxy* to *(∃x)Pyx·(y)Qxy* on the ground that

Pyx is not a function of one variable so that the scope of x is not simply the function *Pyx*. But this is not the case. For the *y* does not fall within the scope of *(y)* since the range of values of *y* are objects, not references to objects. Hence the objection fails. But it fails for yet another and more important reason. We cannot sensibly explain the function of any variable by saying that it, in a context-free way, stands for anything. While it makes some kind of sense to say that *John* stands for John, it makes no sense to say that *y* stands for y. It would be like saying that *that* stands for that, or that *it* stands for it (where of course, we have in mind the relative-pronominal uses of *that* and *it* rather than their demonstrative uses). Hence devices of this sort are of absolutely no avail.

We could, of course, consider singular statements like *love John* or *above $x_1 y_1$* etc. and so construe all relational statements without qualifiers in this way. But the fatal difficulty in this would be that we would thus have no way of expressing the general relational statements such as *$(\exists x)(y)xRy$*. And so it follows that the reduction of dyadic relational facts to pairs of monadic facts is seen to be a fruitless venture.

As a sort of appendix, we might make a few remarks about the so-called Wiener-Kuratowski method of constructing relations out of classes. That this is wholly unsuitable for the philosophical elucidation of relations can be shown as follows. One form of this method consists in the successive construction of a sequence of ordered couples and then treating a relation as a class of such. Thus we have the unit-class of x_1 and the couple class of x_1, y_1, i.e., *$[x_1]$, $[x_1, y_1]$*, and similarly for the ordered couples $x_3, y_2; x_3, y_3$: $x_1 x_3$; etc. The relation, then, is a class of classes of classes:

$$\left\{ \begin{array}{l} [x_1], [x_1, y_1] \\ [x_2], [x_2, y_2] \\ [x_n], [x_n, y_n] \end{array} \right\}$$

Now this construction will enable us to define all the logical properties of relations. But without some additional devices, it will not permit us to differentiate between any two relations which have all their logical properties in common. For instance, if it so happened that all the pairs of things one of which was larger than the other also fulfilled the condition that the larger one of each pair was darker than the smaller one, these different relations could not be represented. If we attempted to correct this by assuming a primitive monadic predicate belonging to the class of classes of classes, not only would this assumption be entirely gratuitous but, worse, we would have no way of explaining how higher-level classes could have primitive undefined properties of the sort required. And so it seems that these additional devices are incoherent. But even if some other unobjectionable one could be discovered, the necessity of using it would thwart the original purpose. For we could have saved all the trouble by introducing dyadic primitive predicates at the outset.

This completes, I think, the argument that dyadic predicates are logically indispensable constituents of an adequate symbolism for describing some of the facts of our world, which is another way of saying that relations are constitutive features of what there is.

Additional note. Lewis and Langford[4] suggest that polyadic relations are reducible to dyadic relatives. The device in question which they probably had in mind was the relative product of two relations. Thus, for example, the triadic relation $B(x,y,z) \equiv (xRy \cdot ySz)$. But it is clear that this generalization should be scrutinized carefully. It might have been that a pair of dyadic relations can always be *constructed* in these cases or that such a pair could always be discovered. The former alternative is only of technical importance, and the latter is very doubtful, albeit of great philosophical interest if true.

4. Ibid.

13

Logic and
the Laws of Nature

The attitudes towards those universal propositions which formulate the routines which men believe constitute the uniformities of experience have undergone radical changes. For a long time these routines were regarded as laws of nature, and this name has remained long after its original significance has been, for the most part, forgotten. And for a long time, in fact for about nineteen centuries, these routines were thought to depend in one way or another on the very principles of logic. The principles of natural science were thus thought to be necessary in the logical sense of the word. An extended proof that this is historically true would be out of place in the present essay. But a careful examination of what Aristotle means by scientific principles reveals that he regards all science as essentially logical in character.

Some criticism of the alleged necessity of natural laws can be found in the writings of the antique sceptics, and further and more consequent doubts were expressed in the Middle Ages in Islam and later in Christendom. The prevailing attitude, however, remained until the time of Hume, who discussed the question more thoroughly than ever before. His results, while well known, have been misunderstood and needlessly confused with the psychological doctrines in

151

which they were stated, and so it is worthwhile to restate them once again.

According to Hume, neither particular causal generalizations nor the general principles (1) that every event has a cause, and (2) that similar causes have similar effects, are guaranteed by logical principles.

From the beginning of formal logic until the time of Hume, the majority of writers on the subject came to agree that a logically necessary proposition is one whose negation is self-contradictory. This view of logic can be retained at the present time if we limit the subject to the so-called sentential calculus. There are some good reasons for doing this which I shall not attempt to justify here. If it is agreed, at all events, that the noncontroversial part of logic consists of theses whose truth can be shown by reducing their negations to self-contradictions, then Hume's point can be sustained. For it is simply that the principles (1) that all events have causes, (2) that similar causes have similar effects, and (3) that any particular given character A is always followed by a certain character B, can be successfully denied without contradiction. We are in a better position than Hume was to make the point perfectly clear, since we have the benefit of the devices of modern logic. And we can see that the statement *(∃x) begins x ·∼(∃y)y causes x* is perfectly free from contradiction. For unless we give to the word *begin* much more than its minimal meaning (i.e., to be after not having been), we can never deduce from *(∃x) begins x* that *(∃y)y causes x*.

Similarly, from the fact that on one occasion an instance of some characteristic A under circumstances D was immediately followed by an instance of a character B, we can never deduce that another instance of A under circumstances D will be followed by another instance of B. Thus qualitative generalizations of the sort are never decidable on formal grounds alone.

The qualitative laws of the less-advanced sciences are empirical synthetic propositions. The same thing is true of quantitative generalizations, although the use of mathematics appears to have misled some people into the belief that this gives a deductive assurance. A recent writer on induction supposes that Hume succeeded only in showing that these maxims are not known to be necessary. This is, I think, a fundamental mistake. Hume's argument shows that these maxims are not necessary in the only clear sense of the word, the formal logical sense of necessary. Others have held that there is some other sense in which such maxims are necessary propositions. But none of the plausible instances of such nonlogically necessary propositions which have been offered are very much like these maxims. Moreover, a careful consideration of such alleged necessities reveals that some of them, at least, are either not necessary or are of the usual variety of analytic propositions of formal logic.

Generalizations about nature, then, are formulable without remainder in terms of what we call truth-functional logic. That is to say, in addition to undefined descriptive predication, all that we need are the usual logical connections, such as conjunction and negation, and some means of generalizing, for instance, *some*. With the minimum of formalism, we can express completely the sense of empirical laws. Such a contention has recently been challenged on the following grounds. A law of nature is ordinarily construed, for example, as follows:

$$(x)\varphi x \supset \psi x$$

or, what is equivalent,

$$\sim(\exists x)\varphi x \cdot \sim \psi x$$

Other qualitative laws are more complex, and further complications are introduced by quantitative laws. But they do not affect, as far as I can see, the main point.

Now it is a well-known theorem that

$$\sim(\exists)\varphi x : \supset : \sim(\exists x)\varphi x \cdot \psi x \cdot \sim(\exists)\varphi x \cdot \sim \psi x$$

And from this it follows that laws of nature whose antecedent conditions are without instances are trivially true. But if this is the case, then the truth-functional logic is insufficient for their expression. The problem has been introduced in recent discussions in terms of the contrary-to-fact conditional statements. We say, for example: "If this vase had been dropped, it would have broken," "If any body were to fall through a vacuum, its acceleration would precisely verify Galileo's principle," etc. Now since these statements mean that the antecedent condition has not been satisfied, it is held that a simple truth-functional analysis of their meaning is impossible.

Many strange consequences have been inferred from this alleged failure of the analytic methods, not the least of which has been the serious proposal to reintroduce pre-Humian views about causal connection. For it is argued as follows: since we can truly say "This vase would break if it were dropped," the vase must now possess a disposition or potency to behave in a specific way even though it does not now exhibit this potency. And because we can truly say "This knife would cut that string if it were drawn across the string," the knife must now possess a disposition or active potency which it does not now exhibit. No positive argument is offered for this conclusion. The negative argument is simply the alleged failure of a truth-functional analysis. And no genuine explanation of active and passive potencies or capacities is given. For it is held that these are primitive notions which must be grasped by a kind of induction (in Aristotle's sense) from particular instances. It will be my purpose in the present essay to examine whether or not a truth-functional analysis of empirical generalization has been decisively eliminated by the so-called problem of the contrafactual conditional.

The first consideration is this: What formal conditions must be fulfilled before we regard a generalization as a law? For it is plain that not every generalization is a law. *All the coins in my pocket are silver* has the form of a generalization, but we would not regard it as a law of nature. In the first place, there is an implicit limitation of time, since, alas, I do not always have coins in my pocket. And secondly, the number of coins that I can carry in my pocket is limited for a variety of reasons. Hence, although *All the coins in my pocket are silver* has a different meaning from *The quarter, the dime, and the two half-dollars are silver*, it is equivalent to this proposition and the further stipulation that these are the only coins in my pocket. No one would regard the latter as a law. In general, when it is known that the antecedent condition determines a finite class whose number does not exceed a fixed n, that decisively eliminates the proposition from the class of laws. We can, then, determine that certain general propositions are not laws, and, I suppose, there are many conditions which are severally required and collectively sufficient conditions constituting the form of a law.

The obvious general conditions required for a proposition to be lawlike are these. If *all A is B* is law-like, then (1) A does not apply to nothing and B does not apply to everything and *A and B* does not involve or constitute a contradiction, and (2) It is not certain that the cardinal number of A's is less than or at most equal to some finite n.

The next thing to be observed is this. An analysis of the meaning of a statement is not, as the phrase "analysis of meaning" misleadingly suggests, the discovery of a hidden treasure. So-called philosophical analysis is actually a reconstruction, i.e., the substitution of a relatively clear statement for a relatively vague one. There is, therefore, no reason to expect, as Mr. Roderick Chisholm seems to do ("The Contrary to Fact Conditional," *Mind*, 55 [1946], first sentence), an indicative statement which will say the same thing as a given contrary-to-fact conditional statement. For in the course of trying to replace a vague statement by a clearer one, we can be forced to employ a conjunction of many statements, at the least. In some instances, we may find that a conjunction alone will not do.

Some preliminary illustrations will show that this is actually the case. Let us take the example suggested to me by Mr. Brian Magee and independently by Professor Gustav Bergmann. *Because he was insulted, he left the conference.* This means *If he is insulted, he leaves the conference, He was insulted* therefore *He left.* This elucidates the application of the rule of inference, because *because* is what grammarians call an illative connective. And so we see that the exposition of a single statement in English involves not only several other English statements but the indication that inference has occurred.

Again consider this: That a number is a prime greater than two implies that the number is odd. Our problem is to explain the meaning of *implies*. Professor G. E. Moore and Professor H. M. Sheffer have independently offered the following elucidation. One statement P "implies" another Q provided that *P and not Q* is self-contradictory, that P is not self-contradictory, that Q is not self-contradictory. This definition of *implies* requires that we understand or can recognize a contradiction when we see one. It also requires that in any particular instance in which the word is employed, the definitions of the words in the implicant and implication are at hand. But it should be clear that we have replaced a single sentence by a fairly complicated series of sentences.

Another point worth observing is that there is no preliminary guarantee that a given artificially constructed language structure is adequate for the clarification of any problem that arises in a natural language. In fact, it is perfectly obvious that we can construct language structures that will be inadequate. Hence, it is always possible that another puzzle arising from the use of natural language will require an alteration or extension of the reconstructed language. Our contention in the present paper is simply that the puzzles presented by the contrary-to-fact conditional can all be resolved without such an alteration and without any extension of the available means of expression in the reconstructed language.

Let me introduce the problem in terms of qualitative laws and then proceed to deal with the more difficult problem of quantitative laws.

The argument, I believe, has the following form. *If this vase had been dropped it would have broken* asserts the indicative conditional *If this vase drops, it breaks* and it asserts the indicative *This vase has not been dropped*. Hence it asserts the conjunction *This vase has not been dropped and if it is dropped it breaks*. To be more exact, it asserts the conjunction *This vase has not been dropped up to the present time and if it is dropped at any time up to the present time, it breaks*. But if we insist that the only functions of statements are truth-functions, then there is nothing else that the contrary-to-fact conditional can assert. Hence it asserts nothing but the aforementioned conjunction. But if so, we can infer the indicative conditional *If this vase is dropped up to the present time it breaks* from the denial of its antecedent *This vase has not been dropped up to the present time*. But, since it is clear that this was not the intended meaning, truth-functional logic is inadequate for the analysis of such contrary-to-fact conditions. As a consequence, there is no difficulty in inferring that a given statement which asserts P and which asserts Q asserts the simple conjunction P *and* Q and nothing else. Now I think that these assumptions cannot be upheld. Before I attack the argument in detail, I shall set forth what I think is the correct analysis of the contrary-to-fact conditional. Then I shall return to the argument.

The clue to the solution of the alleged difficulties is to be found in discovering how we came to believe such conditions and what purposes they serve. I shall propose that a contrary-to-fact conditional expresses not simply the conjunction of the two indicative statements mentioned above but also, implicitly, the existence of evidence on which the indicative statements depend. In other words, it implicitly asserts the belief in the indicative conditional on evidence.

Suppose we consider a parallel case. Suppose I assert an alternative statement, for example, *He is discussing literature or playing chess,* and suppose that I also assert *He is playing chess.* From one point of view I might just as well have asserted simply *He is playing chess.* For from this assertion, *He is discussing literature or playing chess* logically follows. But I ordinarily do not assert and do not believe alternative statements simply because I assert and believe in the truth of one of the alternatives. Thus if I say *If he had not been playing chess he would have been discussing literature,* I surely express belief in *He is playing chess* but I also express an independent and prior belief in *He is discussing literature or playing chess.* The independence and temporal priority of the belief in the alternative statement is, I maintain, a part of what is intended in the contrary-to-fact conditional just mentioned. No attention is paid to the fact that the alternative is also trivially true because one of the alternatives is true. The reason that this is given no attention is not merely ignorance or ignoration of the logical principle $p \supset pvq$. As W. R. Johnson has pointed out, such propositions are quite useless for inference. If I know pvq solely because I know p, such an alternative cannot be employed for inference. Likewise, if I know $p \supset q$ solely because I know $\sim p$ or solely because I know q, $p \supset q$ cannot be used in inference. In fact, only if I have evidence for $p \supset q$ which is independent of any knowledge that $\sim p$ and independent of any knowledge that q, can I use $p \supset q$ for inference. Johnson has explained all this in his *Logic,* and it is not necessary to repeat his arguments here. The habitual users of a natural language behave, I think, as if they were able to avoid certain kinds of nonsense, at least.

When someone says *If this vase had been dropped it would have broken,* he intends to express something like the following: (1) There is evidence *for* and no evidence against the generalization *All vases of this construction, if dropped, break;* (2) In addition, there is subsequent and independent evidence for *This vase has not been dropped.*

Everyone knows, or on a little reflection can discover, what sort of evidence is offered for (1). We believe such statements either because (a) all the vases of the construction in question which are known to have been dropped are known to have broken; or (b) the construction and constitution of such vases is a determinate of the determinable Q and we believe $(x)[(Qx \cdot dropped\ x) \supset breaks\ x]$ on the basis of experiences with *other* determinates of the determinable

Q; or (c) *vase of this construction and constitution* means to us the conjunction of characteristics v_1, v_2 . . .v_n and we believe of a sub-conjunction v_1, . . . v_k of this conjunction that $(x)[v_{1_x} \cdot v_{2_x} \cdots v_{k_x} \supset (dx \supset bx)]$; or finally (d) we have a theory that implies $(y)[(Ky \cdot Sy) \supset By]$ and the empirical correlates of K, S, B are respectively v, d, b, i.e., *vase of this construction*, *dropped*, and *break*. Also it is plain enough how we discover that an object before us is a vase which has not been dropped. Even if we are not conscious of the evidential basis of such convictions, we certainly can bring ourselves to see that some such evidence is presumed when we express such beliefs. We certainly do not have beliefs in conditionals which are true solely because their antecedents are false or solely because their consequents are true.

Let me now return for a moment to the assumptions which lie at the foundation of the argument that truth-functional logic cannot adequately deal with the analysis of contrary-to-fact conditionals. The purpose of analysis is not to give a line-for-line translation of natural language. There is simply no basis for the belief that for every unit of natural discourse there is to be a corresponding unit of the constructed formal language. This would leave out of account all the implicit suggestions and cues of natural language discourse. Such suggestions and cues cannot be literally translated at all, and it is only by learning and habituation that we acquire facility in employing and responding to them. The analytic reconstruction can, however, elucidate them in an indirect way. It does this, not necessarily by way of scientific psychology and scientific linguistics (although these are often of great help), but by a recording of observations of natural usage behavior. Hence we must not expect a simple formal rendering of every kind of statement in natural language.

The assumption that truth-functional logic is not capable of dealing with statements about belief or statements about the relation of evidential statements to conclusions is not well founded. But even if it were, the conclusion that is sometimes drawn is not established. For from the fact that statements occur in contexts that cannot be interpreted in a truth-functional way it does not follow that they express, for example, causal connections between the facts alleged by antecedent and those alleged by consequents of conditional statements. It will be recalled that Hume, although he found more in causal beliefs than the sequences of sensory experiences, did not attribute this additional feature to sensory experience but rather to an impression of reflection. Thus, even if we find that statements occur in contexts that cannot be dealt with in a truth-functional logic, we cannot conclude that the additional features of the context are features of the facts referred to. It is still plausible to suppose that the additional features can be described in terms of the attitudes which we have toward the statements in question. This being a plausible suggestion, the offer of powers, dispositions, or causal connection may, for the time being at least, be declined with thanks.

In any case, the contrary-to-fact conditional *If this vase had been dropped it would have broken* explicitly asserts simply and solely *This vase has not been dropped* and *If this vase is dropped it breaks* does not entail the strange consequences described previously. For as we have seen, it asserts, although implicitly, *I believe that vases of a given sort break if dropped because I have such and such evidence and I later and independently know a vase of the required sort which has not been dropped.* It is perfectly plain that I cannot deduce the objectionable consequences from this statement. In order to see this more clearly I propose the following: If the only possible reason for asserting *If this vase is dropped it breaks* is *This vase has not been dropped,* then of course we can also assert *If this vase is dropped it does not break.* Moreover, if the only possible reason for asserting *Vases of this sort break if dropped* is *No vases of this sort are ever dropped,* then of course we can also assert *Vases of this sort if dropped do not break.* But if these were the only possible reasons for asserting such statements, it is hard to believe that anyone but a formal logician would have made such assertions. Now we know that people who do not know the principles $\sim p \supset p \supset q$, $\sim p \supset p \supset \sim q$, and $\sim\{(\exists x)\varphi x\} \supset \sim\{(\exists x)\varphi x \cdot \sim \psi x\} \cdot \sim \{(\exists x)\varphi x \cdot \psi x\}$ still make such assertions. And so it is plausible to assume that they are, in a single English sentence, attempting to communicate belief in two distinct and independent propositions. If this is the case, there is no difficulty with contrary-to-fact conditional sentences that would indicate either a radical alteration of logic or a return to pre-Humean views about causal connection.

Some of the discussions of contrary-to-fact conditionals are concerned with the difficulty of formulating true laws. I have not discussed these points here for two reasons: I have not sufficiently understood these parts of the discussions, and I do not think they are relevant to the question at issue. Moreover, as I have learned from discussions with Professor William Hay, the problem of formulating generalizations that are true is not a problem for logicians to resolve. From the form of a generalization, it is impossible to decide whether it is true. And again, the logician cannot be held responsible for the fact that so many generalizations are found to be false in fact.

Let us turn our attention now to the quantitative laws of the more-advanced sciences. We must say a few preliminary things about such laws before we attempt to show how they can be dealt with in terms of ordinary truth function.

The simple physical laws have the form $fx=y$ or some analogous form. Now if we study this form, we shall find that the simplest physical law is vastly more complicated than a qualitative law. In a qualitative law we have, essentially, the association of two fixed characteristics A, B in the form *All A is B* (or some analogous form). The quantitative law constitutes an unlimited set, so to speak, of qualitative laws. For any value of the dependent variables is a fixed determinate quantity. And, roughly speaking, a fixed quantity is a universal whose instances all have a transitive and symmetrical relation to a standard or to some multiple or sub-multiple of a standard. Hence, strictly speaking, for $x=n$ we have $y=m$ and then a qualitative law of the form $m_z \supset_z n_z$. Now our quantitative law is a generalization over universal propositions of the form just mentioned. There is some fixed correlation R whose domain consists of the values of the independent variable and whose converse domain consists of values of the dependent variable.

In the second place, we must attempt to see how we obtain ideal quantitative laws, that is, by means of what evidence it occurs to me to formulate them in a certain way. The values of (for simplicity let us say) the two variables in the situation under observation are recorded. Each time we observe we get slightly different values. If we have a great number of readings, we can see that they fluctuate around a single pair of values, or at least around a very narrow range. If we have enough ingenuity and good fortune, we hit upon a function from which values can be deduced that differ from the observed values by small amounts. Otherwise stated, the observed values deviate negligibly and unsystematically from the deduced values. If we neglect these unsystematic deviations, we can say that each pair of our readings confirm a conditional of the form $n_z \supset_z m_z$, where n and m are the two quantities associated with the physical object under consideration. Our general formula implies each of these special formulae of the form just mentioned. The evidence for the special formulae are the readings we get for m when we have already obtained a reading for n in many cases. The evidence for the general formula consists of the evidences for each of the special formulae.

If we want to state a formula which holds ideally, i.e. which holds when values of magnitudes not included in the generalization have been reduced to zero, we must make further experiments which involve the gradual decrease in these extrinsic magnitudes.

Now we cannot be sure that we have reached the zero of such magnitudes. On the contrary, we can be reasonably sure that we have not done so. We can, on the basis of experiment, formulate a law to the following effect: *As the value of B approaches zero, the function of f(A)=D approaches the function of f'(A)=D.* Now while this mode of expression is cumbersome, it does enable us to avoid the paradox of a contrary-to-fact conditional. The evidence for such a law whose form I have just delineated will be a series of experiments in which the values of the magnitude-kind B are successively diminished.

The ideal law is usually stated as follows: *If B is entirely removed, then f'(A)=D.* But we can easily see that the antecedent is contrary to fact. However, it is not necessary to state the case in this way. And, in fact, the way I proposed brings out the kind of evidence on which the so-called ideal laws are based.

Now this calls for two observations. In the first place, practicing scientists perhaps would not put the matter in this way. They would proceed straight to the simple formulation: *If the B's are zero, then f'(A)=D.* In the second place, the actual observations do not provide us with the function $f'(A)=D$ at all. We have, so to speak, to make a very ingenious guess. Do these observations not suggest that our reconstruction of the situation is gratuitous?

It does not seem to me to be so. The same sort of objection could be raised to the assignment of the probability limit of a sequence of events. In both of these cases there are, doubtless, factors involved in the guessing which are neither part of the evidence nor part of the concept which is formulated. The purpose of a logical reconstruction is to provide a logically consistent and adequate account of scientific generalization, and the other factors may be omitted from a consideration of this kind.

I conclude, therefore, that the arguments which were intended to show that contrafactual conditionals require a radical reconstruction of our views about the nature and form of scientific generalizations are unconvincing.

Qualitative laws and quantitative laws can be expressed adequately in terms of the formal language system of *Principia Mathematica*. In the simplest case, such laws are universal propositions or generalizations over universal propositions. In none of this is there any need of new undefined primitives in logic.

14

The Universal Affirmative

Modern logic, as developed by Peirce, Frege, Russell, and more recent authors such as Quine, is intended to do two things: (1) interpret the logical forms of statements, and (2) set forth valid inference paradigms, or (what is exactly parallel to this) set forth logically true theses.

It can be questioned whether *interpretation* is a sufficiently neutral term, because some logicians understood this to mean analysis. Ramsay, however, puts it better when he defines the task to be one of recommending new usages to replace old usages which have produced puzzles, problems, and confusions. The utility of a clarificatory activity carried out along lines that formal logicians have adopted has often been questioned in the past and is under attack at present. The issues are not wholly clear, but it seems that the philosophers who today oppose formal logic altogether as a tool of clarification would prefer to keep philosophy a pure art, whereas the formalists hope to achieve something general which can be used over and over again.

Without aggravating this quarrel or getting involved in the debate, we can make a few things clear which will help in the final resolution.

First, the purpose of Russell, Peirce, et al. was not to propose forms for statements of pure logic or pure mathematics alone. The latter subject was the main interest of Russell and Whitehead in *Principia Mathematica*; but it evidently was not their only concern, because they devote some considerable discussion to the logical forms of nonlogical statements. Second, the charge that such investigations of the forms of statements involves a separation of "matter and form" is, of course, entirely unfounded and rests on a misunderstanding for which Russell's occasional carelessness is responsible in part. Third, these researches are sometimes said to be limited, in their value, to the explanation of the formal sciences. This, too, is quite wrong. The only clear understanding of the problems of induction, statistical inference, and the like has come from the use of the new methods of logic.

The present interpretation of the universal affirmative is this: Statements of the form *All A is B* are to be interpreted as *If anything is A it is B*. The word *thing* which occurs in *anything* is considered to be a pronominal expression: it in no way has any descriptive function by itself. Our definitions are such that the statement *If anything is A it is B* is to mean nothing other than *Nothing is both A and not B*, which in turn means neither more nor less than *It is not the case that: there is that which is A and not B.*[1]

Two remarks are in order here to avoid any possible misunderstanding. (1) The *is* in the expression *There is* is part of the quantifier and, in particular, has no temporal value (as does the present tense of the verb *to be* in English). All indications of time are to be managed by introducing appropriate descriptive terms. (2) The schematic letters A and B may be replaced by *any* constant predicates, as long as the predicate replacing A is of an appropriate logical type with respect to the predicate replacing B.[2] A further point to be mentioned is this: *All A is B* is not of such a form that *all* appropriate replacements of the two predicate letters yield a *logically true* (or *analytic* or *universally valid*) statement.

---

1. This formulation is intended especially to bring out the fact that *thing* is entirely pronominal and can be replaced entirely by grammatical pronouns without gain or loss of meaning.

2. This is an important and not wholly technical point. Regardless of the Russell paradox, substitution of predicates of inappropriate types makes no *L*-sense.

Some replacements, such as the following, do yield logically true statements:

1. Replacing *A* by *not the same as itself*, regardless of what *B* is replaced by, yields *Nothing is both not the same as itself and not B*. This is analytic because it is logically implied by *Nothing is not the same as itself*, since whatever is logically implied by an analytic statement is itself analytic, and *Nothing is not the same as itself* is clearly analytic.

2. Replacing *B* by *is the same as itself*, regardless of what *A* is replaced by, yields *Nothing is A and not the same as itself*, which is analytic.

3. Replacing *A* by *P and Q* (i.e., by any conjunction of adjectives) and *B* by *P* (or by *Q* or by *P or Q*) yields, for example, *Nothing is both P and Q and not P*, which is clearly analytic.

It is clear that many other substitutions will yield nonanalytic statements. Consequently the form adopted for constructing *All A is B* is adequate for all universal affirmative statements, whether they are logically true, logically false, or logically indeterminate (i.e., factual) statements. If it is necessary to specify that any universal affirmative statement is to be understood as nonanalytic, we can do this by explicitly including an explanatory clause to the following effect: *All A_1 is B_1*, and A_1 is not logically empty, B_1 is not logically universal, and A_1 *and not B_1* is not logically empty. It is clear that there is a great difference between saying $(\exists x)A_1x$ and saying $(\exists x)A_1x$ *is not a contradiction*; likewise between saying $\sim(\exists x)\sim B_1x$ and saying '$(\exists x)\sim B_1x$' *is a contradiction*.

All that is needed, in order to insure that a proposition of the form *All A_1 is B_1* is factual or logically indeterminate, is to ascertain that $(\exists x)A_1x$ is logically possible, that $(\exists x)B_1x$ is logically possible, that $(\exists x)A_1x \cdot \sim B_1x$ is logically possible, and finally that at least one descriptive predicate occurs in the predicate A_1 and B_1. It is clear, also, that the conditions under which *All A_1 is B_1* is true or false can be stated even though we are never in position to establish its truth or falsity. *All A_1 is B_1* is true if and only if no singular statement of the form $A_1x_j \cdot \sim B_1x_j$ is true. The fact that this cannot be known does not affect the *definition* of truth.

There are to be, then, some factual[3] statements of the form *All A*

3. *Factual* means only logically indeterminate, i.e., not certifiable on logical grounds alone. Whether a *factual* statement is true or false and whether it is

is B construed as meaning *It is not the case that: there is that which is A and not B*. Such a statement is false if some statement of the form *This A is not B* or *There is an A which is not B* is true; and it is barely acceptable as long as such counter-examples are not *found* (although many other grounds for acceptance or rejection could be invoked, for example that *There is an A which is not B* is deducible from our general stock of accredited scientific statements).

The question now arises as to the meaning of the statement that a given universal affirmative is "about existence." This *may* mean "has existential import." But this latter phrase often is used simply to specify that *There is an A and there is a non-B* is true. There is another sense of "about existence" which needs to be mentioned.

Let *A* be replaced by either (1) a single logically uncompounded predicate *P*, or (2) a logically compound predicate which consists of *Q, R, S,* such that the replacement will be *f(Q,R,S)* where *f* is some logical connective (e.g., *and, or,* etc.). Then, to say that *All A_1 is B_1* is "about existence" is to say that (1) *All A_1 is B_1* is logically indeterminate, and (2) A_1 is a single descriptive predicate or a compound predicate whose constituents are descriptive predicates.

How is this an elucidation of "Such-and-such a statement is about existence"? In this way. It is plausible to suppose that statements are concerned with the factual or the extradiscursive when they are logically indeterminate and when they contain descriptive expressions, that is, expressions whose significance can be ascertained only by reference to some extradiscursive realm. Now all that is required here is that the meaning of the descriptive predicates be *ultimately* ascertained in this way. Thus if the expression A_1 and the expression B_1 are nonlogical constants (i.e., not variables or schematic letters), they may be compounds of descriptive expressions. So in order that statements in which they occur be "about existence" it is necessary and sufficient only that the constituents of such compounds have application to actual occurrences.

To illustrate: *All planets within the orbit of Mercury have a mean surface temperature exceeding 400° F* (for simplicity, assuming that any planet within the orbit of Mercury would undergo no axial rotation). Or *All planets beyond the orbit of Pluto have a mean surface*

---

acceptable or rejectable must depend on extralogical considerations. In particular, its acceptability or rejectability will be in some way dependent on observation and experiment.

temperature less than –300° F. Put *M = being a planet of the solar system within the orbit of Mercury*, *P = being a planet of the solar system beyond the orbit of Pluto*, *G = being a temperature greater than 400° F*, and *L = being a temperature less than –300°F.* Then we are considering the statements *All M is G* and *All P is L.* These simply mean *It is not the case that: there is that which is M and not G* and *It is not the case that: there is that which is P and not L.*

As before we specify the following: (1) *There is that which is M* is *not* either analytic or contradictory; (2) *There is that which is G* is *not* either analytic or contradictory; and (3) *There is that which is M and not G* is not contradictory. Hence, *All M is G* is logically indeterminate. Furthermore *M* and *G* are compound predicates whose *constituents* are known to be instantiated. *But* (we assume) it is not known whether or not *M, G,* etc., are instantiated. Perhaps we should also assume that the stock of knowledge implies neither *There is that which is M* nor *It is not the case that: there is that which is M*, and perhaps likewise for *G, P,* and *L.*

The grounds for accepting *All M is G* are, therefore, not any instances which exemplify *M* and *G*, but rather that *All M is G* is either deducible from our stock of knowledge, including, of course, the principles of celestial mechanics, etc., or at least that our stock of knowledge makes it very probable that *all M is G.*

These examples could be multiplied. A paleontologist once thought that certain tracks in fossil rocks from a certain geological period were made by a heteropod[4] vertebrate (amphibian or reptilian). The following line of reasoning was undoubtedly involved: *All vertebrates at this particular period were either aquatic or ambulatory terrestrial forms*; hence *All heteropod vertebrates at this particular period were either aquatic or terrestrial ambulatory forms.* This deduction is justified by the rule *If all V is A, then indeed, all V is A, so, also, all VH is A.* Notice, however, first, *All VH is A* is not based on examining instances of *VH* (for there may, for all we know, be no instances of *VH*; all we know is that this is not *excluded* by logical or factual considerations). Second, *All VH is A* will be true if *All V is A* is true, even if, later, we discover that there is no *VH.* Third, *All V is A* is not true on logical grounds, for *being a vertebrate at a certain time* does not logically imply *being either aquatic or ambulatory terrestrial.* There is, then, a large class of universal affirmative statements

4. Having the forelimbs of a different structure from the hind limbs.

which cannot be classified as either finite conjunctions of singular statements or as logically certifiable.

It is now to be suggested that when we say that universal statements are "about existence" we may mean the following: (1) The descriptive predicates occurring in the universal statements are either instantiated in fact or they are compound predicates whose constituents are instantiated in fact; (2) The universal statements are logically indeterminate. In many cases, of course, the universals have "existential import." But this can always be made explicit. For example, *All V is A* means *There is a V, and no V is not A*; or, more precisely, $(\exists x)Vx\cdot\sim(\exists x)Vx\cdot\sim Ax$, which means the same as $(\exists x)Vx\cdot(x)Vx \supset Ax$.

We should observe once again that the main part of *All V is A* is negative in its force: it *excludes* the occurrence of that which is *V* is not *A*. The so-called existential import has, by itself, nothing essentially to do with the universal statement being "about existence." To show this, notice the following: Put *I* for *is the same as* and consider *All things are self-identical*, i.e., $(x)Ixx$, i.e., $\sim(\exists x)Ixx$. We have also $(\exists x)Ixx$. But it is questionable, at least, whether *All things are self-identical* is "about existence," although it is not questionable that *All things are self-identical* has existential import. Or, to take a more complex example, *All transitive and symmetrical relations are reflexive*. This has existential import because *There is a transitive and symmetrical relation* is true. (Logical identity is transitive and symmetrical.) Again, *All asymmetrical and one-many relation are intransitive* has import because there are asymmetrical and one-many relations. (*Father of, immediate predecessor in the natural number series,* etc., are asymmetrical and one-many.) Thus, "existential import" used to mean that the subject-term of a universal affirmative proposition has instances, is not necessarily connected with being "about existence." On the other hand, universal affirmatives can be "about existence" without having "existential import." There is, therefore, an important distinction to be made between the general use of *There is that which is . . .* and a very special use of this expression. The special use of this expression is exhibited by the fact that some predicates of our discourse gain their meaning only from some application which is empirical. In other words, what exists empirically is exhibited by our undefined descriptive predicates $P_1 \ldots P_n$, for they can only be used provided that at least one sentence containing each of them, of the form *There is that which is P_j*, is true. This is the main "point of contact" between discourse and fact. All the compound descriptive predicates can be significantly used regardless of whether they have application or not, provided only that they have been compounded "properly" (i.e., that they have been compounded according to the rules of logical syntax).

For the purposes of this discussion it does not matter what we choose as undefined descriptive predicates. *House, dog,* etc., are the undefined descriptive predicates in the language of the child. All that matters is that we see how these predicates are used by a given language user. The logical inferences we make all obey the same rules (with systematic ambiguity, of course).

The previous discussion has little to do with philosophy. What little philosophy there is in it is the tacit assumption that our logic is to be two-valued (a multivalued logic has no satisfactory interpretation in terms of truth-values), and that some descriptive predicates derive their meaning empirically.

REFERENCE MATTER

A Bibliography
of the Writings
# of Julius R. Weinberg

BOOKS

An Examination of Logical Positivism. International Library of
Psychology, Philosophy and Scientific Method. London: Kegan
Paul, Trench, Trubner and Co., and New York: Harcourt, Brace
and Co., 1936. Reprinted in papberback by Littlefield, Adams
and Co., Paterson, New Jersey, 1960. Translated into Italian
(1950) and Spanish (1959).

Nicolaus of Autrecourt: A Study in Fourteenth-Century Thought.
Princeton: Princeton University Press, 1948. Reprinted by Greenwood Press, New York, 1969.

A Short History of Medieval Philosophy. Princeton: Princeton University Press, 1964. Hardcover and paperback.

Abstraction, Relation, and Induction. Madison: University of Wisconsin Press, 1965.

Ideas and Concepts. Milwaukee: Marquette University Press, 1970.
The 1970 St. Thomas Aquinas Lecture.

Problems in Philosophical Inquiry. New York: Holt, Rinehart and
Winston, 1971. Issued in hardcover (one volume) and in paperback (four volumes). Edited with Keith E. Yandell.

ARTICLES IN JOURNALS

"Are There Ultimate Simples?" *Philosophy of Science*, 2 (1935),
387-94.

173

"A Possible Solution of the Heterological Paradox." *Philosophical Review*, 46 (1937), 657-59.

"Studia Philosophica: Discussion." *Philosophical Review*, 47 (1938), 70-77.

"On 'This is white'." *Philosophical Review*, 50 (1941), 317-20.

"Ockham's Conceptualism." *Philosophical Review*, 50 (1941), 523-28.

"The Fifth Letter of Nicholas of Autrecourt to Bernard of Arezzo." *Journal of the History of Ideas*, 3 (1942), 220-27.

"Our Knowledge of Other Minds." *Philosophical Review*, 55 (1946), 555-63.

"Nicholas of Autrecourt: A Reply [to E. A. Moody]." *Journal of Philosophy*, 46 (1949), 817-22.

"The Idea of Causal Efficacy." *Journal of Philosophy*, 47 (1950), 397-407.

"Contrary-to-fact Conditionals." *Journal of Philosophy*, 48 (1951), 17-22.

"Concerning Allegedly Necessary Nonanalytic Propositions." *Philosophical Studies*, 2 (1951), 17-20. Written with William H. Hay.

"Concerning Undefined Descriptive Predicates of Higher Levels. *Mind*, 63 (1954), 338-44.

"*Cogito, Ergo Sum*: Some Reflections on Mr. Hintikka's Article." *Philosophical Review*, 71 (1962), 483-91.

"The Novelty of Hume's Philosophy." *Proceedings and Addresses of the American Philosophical Association*, 38 (1965), 17-35. The Western Division Presidential Address.

CONTRIBUTIONS TO BOOKS

"David Hume." In *A Dictionary of Philosophy*, edited by D. D. Runes, p. 132. New York: Philosophical Library, 1942. Reprinted by Littlefield, Adams and Co., Paterson, New Jersey, 1955.

"Logical Positivism." In *American Philosophy*, edited by Ralph B. Winn, pp. 183-91. New York: Philosophical Library, 1955.

"The Fifth Letter of Nicolas of Autrecourt to Bernard of Arezzo." In *Inquiries into Medieval Philosophy*, edited by James F. Ross, pp. 315-24. Westport, Connecticut: Greenwood Publishing Co., 1971.

"On Sabine's Philosophy of Value." In *Essays in Political Theory*, edited by M. R. Konvitz and A. E. Murphy, pp. 246-56. Ithaca, New York: Cornell University Press, 1948. Reprinted by Kennikat Press, Port Washington, New York, 1971.

"The Problem of Sensory Cognition." In *Essays on Knowledge and Method*, edited by Edward D. Simmons, pp. 29-40. Milwaukee: Ken Cook Publishing Co., 1965.

"Nicolas of Autrecourt." In *Encyclopedia of Philosophy*, edited by Paul Edwards, pp. 499-502. New York: The Macmillan Company, 1965.

"A Brief Comment on Gregory's Critique." In *Problems in Philosophical Inquiry*, edited with Keith E. Yandell, Vol. IV, pp. 8-9. New York: Holt, Rinehart and Winson, 1971.

"Abstraction in the Formation of Concepts." In *Dictionary of the History of Ideas*, Vol. I, pp. 1-9. New York: Charles Scribner's Sons, 1973.

"Causation." In *Dictionary of the History of Ideas*, Vol. I, pp. 270-78.

REVIEWS

K. Popper, *Logik der Forschung*. In *Philosophical Review*, 45 (1936), 511-14.

J. Schachter, *Prolegomena zu einer kritischen Grammatik*. In *Philosophical Review*, 46 (1937), 334-35.

H. Reichenbach, *La Philosophie Scientifique*. In *Philosophical Review*, 46 (1937), 452.

E. Vouillemin, *La Logique de la science*. In *Philosophical Review*, 46 (1937), 453.

M. Schlick, *Sur la fondement de la connaisance*. In *Philosophical Review*, 46 (1937), 453.

R. Carnap, *Le Problème de la logique de la science*. In *Philosophical Review*, 46 (1937), 563-64.

J. Pacotte, *La Logique et l'empirisme integral*. In *Philosophical Review*, 48 (1939), 84-85.

R. I. Aaron, *John Locke*. In *Philosophical Review*, 49 (1940), 83-85.

Studia Philosophica, vol. II. In *Philosophical Review*, 49 (1940), 364-68.

Six Review Abstracts in *Philosophical Abstracts*, 1 (1940).

R. Carnap, *Foundations of Logic and Mathematics*; L. Bloomfield, *Linguistic Aspects of Science*; John Dewey, *Theory of Valuation;* and Joseph Woodger, *The Technique of Theory Construction*. In *Kenyon Review*, 2 (1941), 489-93.

Richard von Mises, *Kleines Lehrbuch der Positivismus*. In *Philosophical Review*, 51 (1942), 331-35.

Ockham, *Tractatus de Successivis*. In *Philosophical Review*, 54 (1945), 519-20.

Ockham, *Tractatus de Praedestinatione*. In *Philosophical Review*, 55 (1946), 446-48.

Giles of Rome, *Errores Philosophorum*, ed. J. Jochnin. In *Philosophical Review*, 54 (1945), 619-21.

M. J. Grajewski, *Formal Distinction of Duns Scotus.* In *Philosophical Review*, 55 (1946), 448-49.

Duns Scotus, *De Primo Principio.* In *Philosophical Review*, 60 (1951), 107-9.

Freedom and Reason: Essays Presented to Morris R. Cohen. In *Judaism*, 1 (1952), 286-88.

Buescher, *The Eucharistic Teaching of William of Ockham.* In *Philosophical Review*, 62 (1953), 652-53.

A. C. Crombie, *Robert Grosseteste.* In *Modern Schoolman*, 31 (1954), 325-27.

Philotheus Boehner, *Medieval Logic: An Outline of Its Development.* In *Scripta Mathematica*, 20 (1955), 184-86.

Nicolaus Cusanus, *Of Learned Ignorance*, translated by G. Heron. In *New Scholasticism*, 29 (1955), 342-44.

John of Salisbury, *The Metalogicon*, translated by Daniel D. McGarry. In *Philosophical Review*, 66 (1957), 559-61.

S. M. Afnan, *Avicenna, His Life.* In *Philosophical Review*, 69 (1960), 255-59.

Gordon Leff, *Medieval Thought.* In *Philosophical Review*, 69 (1960), 419-22.

Robert McRae, *The Problem of the Unity of the Sciences from Bacon to Kant.* In *American Historical Review*, 68 (1963), 411-12.

Armand Maurer, *Medieval Philosophy.* In *Philosophical Review*, 72 (1963), 536-38.

E. Gilson and T. Langan, *Modern Philosophy.* In *Philosophical Review*, 75 (1966), 110-13.

TRANSLATIONS

In M. G. Singer and R. R. Ammerman, eds., *Introductory Readings in Philosophy*, pp. 185-91. New York: Charles Scribner's Sons, 1962. *Summa Theologica*, Part I, Question 2, Article Three.

In Julius R. Weinberg and Keith E. Yandell, eds., *Problems in Philosophical Inquiry*. New York: Holt, Rinehart and Winston, 1971. Descartes: pp. 43-44 (from Meditation Two, AT VII, 24^{14}-25^{18}; *Reply to Fifth Set of Observations*, AT VII, 352); p. 100 (from *Meditation Six*, AT VII, 79^{5}-80^{30}); p. 284 (from *Meditation Six*, AT VII, 78^{1}-78^{20}); pp. 312-13; (from Letters to Princess Elizabeth, May 31 and June 28, 1643). Leibniz: pp. 100–101 (from *Critical Remarks Concerning Descartes' Principles*); p. 314 (*Discourse on Metaphysics*, Section 14). Anselm: pp. 498-99 (from *Proslogian*, chs. 2 and 3). Gregory of Rimini: pp. 499-500 (from *Questions on the First Book of the Sentences*, Distinctions 42-44, edition of 1522, folio 70 ff.).

Index of Names

DESIGNED BY IRVING PERKINS
COMPOSED BY THE BLUE RIDGE GROUP, LTD.,
EAST FLAT ROCK, NORTH CAROLINA
MANUFACTURED BY THOMSON-SHORE, INC., DEXTER, MICHIGAN
TEXT IS SET IN PRESS ROMAN, DISPLAY LINES IN FRITZ QUADRATA

ꟼꟼ

Library of Congress Cataloging in Publication Data
Weinberg, Julius Rudolph, 1908-1971.
Ockham, Descartes, and Hume.
"A Bibliography of the writings of Julius R.
Weinberg": p.
Includes index.
1. Philosophy—Addresses, essays, lectures.
2. Ockham, William, d. ca. 1349—Addresses, essays,
lectures. 3. Descartes, René, 1596-1650—Addresses,
essays, lectures. 4. Hume, David, 1711-1776—Addresses,
essays, lectures. I. Title.
B29.W4145   190   76-11315
ISBN 0-299-07120-0